TABLE
for
ONE

A SINGLE'S JOURNEY FROM
BITTERNESS TO CONTENTMENT

BEN PUKAS

Cover Designer: Rony Dhar
Interior Layout Designer: Osamudiamen Abdul

Library of Congress Cataloging-in-Publication Data
ISBN: 979-8-218-63227-4

Printed in the United States of America

Contents

To my single friends…there's purpose and hope.

Introduction

"How Many in Your Party?"

I'm currently sitting in a coffee shop in Little Rock, Arkansas, at my table for one, nostalgically staring out the window and wondering how the heck I got here. The Ben Pukas who started writing this book is not the same Ben Pukas who is sitting in this coffee shop. It doesn't feel like I have finished a book. It feels like the end of a very lengthy, very worthwhile journey.

Let's flashback to January 2020. I had just preached a sermon on singleness that struck a nerve in our church. Most of our people had never heard of singleness as a gift. The sermon was revolutionary for so many people.

After the sermon a key member came up to me with the lead pastor and said, "Ben, I'm not kidding you when I say this, but I think you should write a book on singleness from the perspective of a single guy."

I mean the concept was laughable. I hated writing. It made me feel nauseous and gross. I also didn't want to be the single pastor who wrote a singleness book because he was single. No thanks, I'll take literally any other cliché. Plus, I wouldn't be single long enough to write said book.

Even though I had just preached a sermon on the gift of singleness, I felt like it was anything but a gift. I was struggling to find meaning. I couldn't understand how a loving Father could actively give his children singleness. Really, I couldn't understand how God had given *me* singleness.

But God did what he does best: he was so patient with me, but he never yielded. I said no for more than five months. "Pick someone else, God. I'm not your guy." However, God won the wrestling match, and I finally decided to be faithful. I didn't start writing this book to be a published author; I started writing because I was grasping for straws and longing for answers. I realized I didn't want to write, not because I was desperately trying to avoid the cliché, but because I didn't want to have to look in the mirror.

I hated my singleness more than I hated writing. I wasn't just bitter about my singleness; I was bitter toward the church. I loved my job, but Sunday mornings were really hard for me. I didn't like being single, and it felt as if the church was always reminding me of my relationship status.

A couple of Sundays before the sermon on singleness, I was really struggling with this "oh, so precious gift." I watched the couples walking into church as they held hands, walking close together to stay warm in the cold weather.

It was the Christmas season, which is my favorite time of the year, and all I wanted for Christmas was to watch Christmas movies every night and a person to watch them with me. Christmas was getting closer by the day, but the person I was watching Christmas movies with was my single male roommate. Don't get me wrong. I loved my roommate, but I was very content to watch these movies with him on the other side of the room.

As the couples were filing into church that Sunday morning, sadness and discontentment started to take me over. You know the kind of sadness that makes breathing hurt? I greeted people by putting on the mask so many single people have to put on to get through a Sunday morning church service. We say everything is fine while the world around us feels as if it's on fire.

Then the inevitable happened. Some of you can probably see where this is going. Some of you may feel like I'm telling one of your stories. A rock star of a lady at church asked me if there was anyone special I would be bringing home to meet the family this year. Why that's the first question that comes to people's minds, I will never know.

On the outside I was calm and said, "No ma'am. No girl is that lucky this year," but on the inside there were *other* words I felt.

I walked into the worship center, and not three minutes later I was asked the same question. Are these people in some sort of group text? That Sunday I had to tell people multiple times I wasn't bringing home anybody special or spending the holidays with a special someone. By the end of the morning, you could say I felt anything but special myself.

This story is common. Discouraged is a common emotion single people feel, and discouraged perfectly described how I felt.

I didn't know when I said yes to writing this book that I was saying yes to a journey. A journey that would forever change my life.

I'm now sitting in this Little Rock coffee shop with a smile on my face as the memories of the last four years dance around in my head. That Ben Pukas seems light-years away.

I'm thinking about the gallons of coffee I drank at various shops while writing on a topic I knew little to nothing about and wanting it so badly not to be true about me.

I'm thinking about all the loneliness, bitterness, frustration, hurt, and wrestling I did with God.

I'm thinking about the four breakups; my best friend and roommate getting married; three new roommates moving in and then moving out; and my job title changing from student pastor to lead pastor in the midst of some very uncomfortable turmoil.

To say it was a tough four years would be an understatement.

And do you know what's crazy? I wouldn't trade that time for anything. Yes, it was hard, but in the midst of it all, Jesus was all I had a lot of times. He was the only one I could turn to. My quiet times during the last four years have been full of tears, questions and the occasional cuss word, but they have been so sweet, so real, and so deep.

I wrote this book from the reality of being single. Yes, I'm okay, and no, I don't need you to set me up with your friend from work who just happens to be single and surprisingly perfect for me, even though we just met thirty-seven seconds ago. I get to say all the cliché things your married friends say *and* sit in the uncomfortable awkwardness with you after I say it. I'm right there with you. *Just because singleness may make us feel a certain way, it doesn't make the promises of God any less true, put God any less in control or make singleness any less a good and perfect gift.*

As you read this book, you will see how my heart changed over time. The other day I went back and read through the first few chapters and felt as if I were going back and reading my journal from junior high. I could see the bitterness and frustration. I was going to edit it out, but I decided not to.

When you read the book of Psalms, especially the ones David wrote, there's a lot of rawness there. God didn't edit all the honesty out. It was real. It was how he was feeling at the time. Just because we follow Jesus doesn't mean we're going to love every situation we're in. And there are times I read those real and raw verses and I say, "Me too, David. Me too." And this guy who wrestled with God and felt all these feelings was someone who God said was a man after his own heart.

We're not called to be fake. We're called to live in the light. And that's what I want this book to be for you. I want you to see the transformation. Many of the quotes in this book are copied straight from my journal with God. They are real and raw and some of them may even cause you to wonder how the heck the publisher allowed them to make the final cut of the book. But I also believe the quotes will cause you to relate in a real way to a feeling or a circumstance. You may have had those exact thoughts recently or even have the same thoughts as you're reading. I don't want to dress everything up and make it look nice, because singleness a lot of the time is anything but clean and manageable. I want you to see where I'm at and where I've been and say, "Me too, Ben. Me too."

This book isn't going to give you a list of ten things you need to do to find contentment in your singleness. Tips and tricks won't bring you contentment. It's not the journey that led me to contentment; it's who was leading me on this journey.

Here's my prayer for you: as I have gone on this journey from bitterness to contentment in the writing of this book, I pray you would be able to go on the same journey as you read it. Not by yourself. With me. With our Jesus.

You're not alone in this. You're not the only one struggling with loneliness and the sting found in the wake of a breakup. You're not the only one who is discouraged. The journey is scary. There will be moments you feel all the feelings, but hang in there. It's hard, but, my friend, it's so worth it. Are you ready to begin the journey? Are you ready to not just know singleness as a gift but truly believe it is? Get cozy at your table for one. Here we go.

Chapter 1

Searching for Something in the Palm of Your Hand

Have you ever lost something really important? Better question. *When* was the last time you lost something really important? Wallet? Phone? Keys? Your mind?

When you lose something, there's a moment when you realize you lost it. Your heart skips a few beats, your stomach does a few flips, your breathing intensifies, and the most outrageous, unrealistic scenarios play out in your mind.

When I was in college my parents bought me a new phone. The second I got the phone I put it in a case and made a vow that I would love and cherish it till death do us part. Finals week rolled around. At this point, I'm tired, stressed, and very sleep deprived. I'm in line to get a bite to eat in between tests, and I do the triple pat down to make sure everything is present and accounted for. Wallet—check. Keys—check. Phone—*phone?* My heart skipped a beat and my stomach did a flip. My phone was gone. This is it. This is how I die.

I walked around the food court frantically, probably looking a lot like I had just lost my mind. I'm freaking out, and my dad can sense it.

"Ben, is everything okay?"

"Yes, Dad, everything is fine," I lied. Everything definitely wasn't fine; my life was flashing before my eyes. But I wasn't about to tell him I lost the phone he literally just bought me a few days ago. I wasn't mentally prepared to receive the famous dad speech about being more responsible.

I ran to every table in the food court and asked strangers if they had seen an iPhone in a white case.

How is this possible? Not one person had seen it. And they were looking at me like I was crazy.

"Why are you looking at me like that?"

"You stole it, didn't you?"

Fear was being replaced by paranoia, and everyone was a suspect. Fight or flight. Someone somewhere had seen it.

My dad at this point was obviously concerned and was asking a lot of questions. Questions I was just ignoring. I couldn't take it anymore; I had to put all my attention into finding the phone.

"Dad,"—big sigh, the world is ending—"I lost my phone. I'm going to have to call you back." I hung up the phone. My phone.

The iPhone in the white case. I didn't know whether to laugh, cry, throw up, or take a nap. I was searching for something that was in the palm of my hand the entire time.

These kinds of stories always crack me up, especially when they happen to someone else. It's a perfect mix of stupidity and "laugh at my pain" humor. You search for your sunglasses while they hide on the top of your head. You search for your keys and you're cursing them as if they got up, ran away, and hid themselves, and now they're going to make you late. The audacity! And they are in your hand the whole time.

We search for something in marriage that is easily made available to us now in our singleness.

As a single pastor, it's easy for me to point a finger at married people and blame them for creating this culture, but I have to admit I am just as much a part of this culture as anybody else. Even now I typed the words "single pastor" and immediately felt like a loser. I instantly worried that people would think there's something wrong with me. I've heard those words before, and now, every time I talk about my singleness, I fear I'll hear those words again.

There are some seasons in my life when I absolutely love being single, and there are seasons in my life when I would give just about anything for God to "hurry up and bring my future wife along." Goodness, there are some days I wake up content but then go to bed a disgruntled and frustrated single man.

I am somebody who desires to be married, and there is nothing wrong with that desire. God created marriage to be a good thing

(Prov. 18:22), but he never created it to be ultimate. I can get so caught up on looking for my future wife that I miss the blessings of today. I know God's gift for me right now is singleness, but knowing is different than believing. I feel as if the desires I have now won't be fulfilled until I'm married, and this leads to an obsession of doing everything in my power to find someone to spend the rest of my life with so my life can begin. Every pretty girl I see walk through the doors of the church represents my possible ticket out of singleness. And I know I'm not the only single person who thinks this way. But the church, a lot of the time, reenforces this idea.

A few days ago, I had a friend send me an interview from a Christian radio station. The caption of the text was, "When are you going to be done with the singleness book *upside-down smiley face*?" In this interview they were talking to a megachurch pastor who had just written a book about relationships. One of the hosts was older and single, and the pastor said, "Think how good of a husband you'll be when you get married. Your singleness has been preparing you for that moment."

I had to take a thirty-second time-out. I couldn't believe what he said. I was ready for the hosts to shut the interview down. I was ready for someone to put this man on blast. Honestly, I was ready for someone to open their dang Bible. None of that happened. Instead, the pastor was met with amens and hallelujahs and, "That's the message we need to be getting out. Preach it."

After I was done banging my head on the table and taking a couple shots of Pepto Bismol, it hit me how deep-rooted this issue is. I was frustrated with the interview as a whole but specifically with the pastor who was communicating this.

"Bro, if you would just open your Bible, you would see the benefits of singleness, and that life is way more than just waiting for a spouse."

But I was more frustrated with how I do this very thing in my own singleness. It was as if God just gently tapped me on the shoulder and said, "Ben, when you have those exact same thoughts on *your* singleness, how often do you open your Bible?"

When the Bible talks about singleness, it never alludes to the fact that singleness is just a season that's purpose is to prepare for a future season. Never. Not once. Can it be a byproduct? Absolutely. But is it the main purpose? Absolutely not.

When we make marriage the purpose for singleness, we commu-nicate that marriage is better than singleness. We communicate to single people they haven't quite made it yet. Let me tell you something that may blow your mind: the Bible doesn't teach that. It teaches the opposite. You ready for this? Jesus says in Matthew 19 that *singleness is better than marriage* (Matt. 19:12). Instead of a season that is built to prepare us for marriage, the Bible paints a completely different picture. The Bible is clear on the purpose of singleness.

Singleness is a gift (1 Cor. 7:7). Singleness allows us to be fully devoted to the Lord without the distractions of a partner (1 Cor. 7:32–35). God's purpose for our lives isn't for us to find a spouse; his purpose for our lives is for us to learn to love him with all of our heart, soul, strength, and mind (Luke 10:27) and to love people the way he has loved us (John 13:34–35). And here's the genius plan of God, the time in our lives where we can do that *most effectively* is, drum roll please, in our singleness. You want to be fully devoted to the Lord? You want to learn to love him and love people most effectively? Stay single. Don't get married. How many sermons are preached and how many books have been written that say that?

Running to Marriage or from Singleness?

We put such an emphasis on marriage because we think it's what will fulfill us. We think what we're searching for is in the palm of someone else's hand. The problem isn't that single people are running into a loving union with a husband or a wife; the problem is that single people are running away from singleness as if marriage will solve their loneliness and end their search for love. In other words, marriage isn't something we run *to*, but singleness is something we run *from*. Singleness is a problem that needs fixing and marriage is the prescription. We're searching everywhere for a love that's right in the palm of our hand.

Marriage was created by God to be good, but it can never bear the weight we put on it. We're looking for somebody to complete us and make all things right. We're looking for an iPhone in a white case while we're holding an iPhone in a white case.

We're searching for somebody to love us. "But God shows his love for us that while we were still sinners, Christ died for us" (Rom. 5:8).

We're searching for somebody to make us not feel so alone. "And behold, I am with you always, to the end of the age" (Matt. 28:20).

We're searching for someone to make us feel like we belong. "But you are . . . a people for his own possession. . . . Once you were not a people, but now you are God's people" (1 Peter 2:9–10).

We want someone to rescue us. "He has delivered us from the domain of darkness and transferred us to the kingdom of his beloved son" (Col. 1:13).

I can do this all day, and I'm not saying that arrogantly because I missed my calling as a lawyer. *We all have a longing for someone to win our hearts, but somebody already has. All of our longings are fulfilled in Jesus.* That's why I can do this all day. The question is this: Do we believe that? Do I believe that? No, really. Ask yourself if you really, truly believe that, because I know it but have a very hard time believing it at times. I know it can feel like the Jesus juke of the century, but it needs to be said and then repeated and then preached every second of every day to us. Maybe then it will take that eighteen-inch journey from our head to our heart.

When we run as fast as we can toward marriage, we don't take time to fix our eyes on the one who is the fulfillment of all our longings. We, instead, put our focus on a flawed human being we unrealistically believe is. Again, there's nothing wrong with marriage, but when we fix our eyes on the earthly and take our eyes off of the eternal, that's when there's a problem (Col.

3:2–3). Our future and hope and security aren't with a spouse; that's earthly, therefore it has an end date.

There's a problem. We don't view singleness the way God does. We don't view single *people* the way God views single people, and single people, we don't view ourselves the way God views us. And because of this tragic problem, we are forcing single people to miss out on their purpose *now* because they are too focused on a hypothetical future. Instead of pursuing Jesus, single people are on a mission to pursue a relationship and miss the blessing altogether.

This problem needs to be addressed, and single people, this isn't just our problem. *This is the church's problem.*

Church-Wide Problem, Church-Wide Solution

The question you may be asking yourself is this: How is this the church's problem? Isn't this a book written to single people? The quick answer to that is, yes, it is, but if it stops there, then the problem we have with our worldview on singleness will never change. Single people aren't the only ones who idolize marriage. There is an obvious pressure for single people to hurry the heck up and get out of their singleness, a pressure applied by single people *and* the church.

When I arrived at the church I work at now, many of them were confused how I was in ministry and didn't have a wife. "Wow, it has to be hard to be in full-time ministry and not have the support of a partner." From the moment I arrived there was pressure to find a wife. Everyone was onboard and on a mission to help me find my special someone. They loved me so well, but when it came to my singleness, they weren't loving me well, in fact, they were discouraging me from living out of my gift.

It took a few months to figure out why such an awesome church sucked so bad at singleness, but I came to the conclusion this wasn't done out of spite. Just like the universal church, my church had a worldview problem. *They didn't see singleness as a gift because they didn't know it was a gift.*

You see, if we just speak to single people about singleness, then the problem will never be solved. Singleness is mostly ever preached about in single ministries on Tuesday nights. Most single people leave feeling empowered, encouraged, and ready to use their gift of singleness for the kingdom of God. These people are on fire and nothing can put it out. Nothing. That is until they go home and talk to their parents or, worse, until they go to church the following Sunday morning.

"Are you dating anyone yet?"

"Anyone you got your eye on?"

"Whatever happened to that person you were dating a few months ago? I would like grandkids before I die!"

The point is this: the fire coursing through their veins the week before has not just been extinguished, but the likelihood of starting another fire in the near future is gone as quickly as it was kindled. Their focus shifts from their gift to their future.

The motives behind this aren't evil. The church isn't trying to discourage or crush the spirits of single people, but just because there aren't bad motives doesn't make it right or okay. The old adage is as true today as it was when it was first said: The road to hell is paved with good intentions. This conversation about singleness is way overdue in the church.

Back to this problem at my church. Being the only single male pastor on staff, I entered into conversations with the leadership about this. I entered into these conversations not blaming or pointing a finger but just wanting to help educate and offer the perspective of a single person.

They asked me to speak on it from the stage on a Sunday. They recognized the church needed to be a part of the solution. I was able to shed light on how our body had been trying to love single people but in reality was discouraging them. I opened up God's Word and preached the truth about the gift of singleness that shouldn't be endured but embraced. It was a huge moment for our church. Our single people, some said for the first time ever, left church feeling empowered in their singleness, and our married people felt more equipped in how they could love the single people in their lives.

Galatians 6:2 tells us to "bear one another's burdens." The church needs to be equipped on singleness, not to just avoid being a discouragement, but to actively be an encouragement. There are many times singleness will be hard, and we will ask God if he kept the receipt or if we could regift it to someone else. During those moments we need to be reminded by our church family of the truth of what God thinks of us and our situation. We need people to bear the burden with us. To remind us of our purpose now, not the empty promise of marriage in the future.

Single people, don't allow frustration to lead to bitterness toward your married friends. I say this because it is very easy for me to do. I have recently allowed bitterness to hurt a lot of the people who are close to me. The aim of our charge should be to love whether people understand or not (1 Tim. 1:5). Start a conversation. Ask people for permission to tell them when you don't feel like they're loving you well. Give them practical ways they can love you in your singleness.

We must work together as a church to solve this age-old problem. This isn't going to be easy and mistakes will be made. We have to be patient and realize this will take some time (1 Thess. 5:14).

The Church Is Failing Singles

This book has weighed heavy on my heart. I have met too many people who have the gift of singleness but feel like second-class Christians. They struggle to find a place in their singleness, not necessarily because there isn't a place for them, but because they don't feel as if they belong. I see people like this every time I look in the mirror.

The world is ruthless on its mission to throw its expectations at us. That's no shock to anyone. But what has been shocking to me is that, in the place where the world's expectations are supposed to come and die, they stay and thrive.

As the world feeds us lies, the church needs to remind us that our identity isn't found in what the world wants us to find our identity in. There are countless times I believed the lies of the world as if they were reality, but people came alongside and pointed me back to the truth. That saved me from a whole lot of hurt and pain.

But when it comes to singleness, the church beats the same rhythm on the same drum that the world does. At times, it feels as if the church's beat is louder than the world's beat. Let's pause for a second. Think about it. The world is constantly feeding us lies, and God uses his people to constantly point us back to him. How beautiful is that? How genius is that? But when it comes to singleness, when it comes to single people, they are being told by the world they are missing something if they aren't sharing life with Mr. or Miss Perfect, and then they step through the doors of the church and it's not refuted. It's shouted even louder.

Ouch. I feel that. Can you?

It's not fun. It sucks at times. As every birthday passes, it's another reminder that what I long for most didn't happen that year. I question my worth. I question my standards and if they're too high. But sadly, sometimes I question God. "Do you really see me? Why would you make marriage a good thing but keep it from me? Am I doing something wrong? Should I have given so-and-so another chance? Was that my one shot at love? God, will you *ever* bring anyone?"

And the times I needed to be reminded that my identity isn't found in a spouse (1 Peter 2:9; Gal. 3:27–28), my singleness is a gift (1 Cor. 7:7), and I am God's gift to the church (also 1 Cor. 7), the church either remained deafeningly silent or led me to believe my only purpose was to get ready for the "next season."

Church, the cost is too high to get this wrong.

My biggest prayer is for everyone, especially single people, to realize the love they are searching for so frantically is right in front of them. For people to realize that we are in desperate need of saving, that we are dead in our sin with no hope for a future, but God intervened and saved us (Eph. 2:4–5). The love we're looking for can be found in Jesus and can never be found in a spouse who is just as sinful as we are. What we're looking for is right in the palm of our hands.

Single people, you are valued (Eph. 5:10), you've been bought with a price (1 Cor. 6:19–20), you have a purpose beyond waiting for a future season, and you're going to be okay.

No, *we're* going to be okay. But we have to get this right. Because there's more at stake than just the way we view a relationship status.

Chapter 2

More at Stake than Perspective

I have a motto that can make life very interesting: "Do it for the story." I live and one day I will probably die by that motto. For some reason I get a thrill for the cringeworthy. We all have that friend, and I'm proud to say I'm that friend.

Before I moved to Searcy, Arkansas, I was trained at Watermark Community Church in Dallas, Texas, and let me tell you, Watermark knew how to party. Not the "get crunk" kind of party, but the "do the craziest things and then compare stories later" kind of party. We were about to take off to a staff retreat, and, as always, there was a game involved. Everyone was grouped into cars of people they didn't know very well, and those were the people you would carpool with on the way to the retreat and the people who would be on your team for the game.

The rules of the game were simple: do something crazy with your car on the way up, record it, and send it in. That's it. When we got to the retreat, we would watch all the videos together as a staff and vote on our favorites and our least favorites. Here's the catch, you weren't trying to win, you were just trying not to lose. If you lost, you and your team would have to do something incredibly embarrassing and awkward at a later date and time. Translation, do whatever it takes not to lose. Some of you are hyperventilating. Yeah, so were some of the staff members.

I met my team and we quickly made a plan. We were going to stage a marriage proposal in the food court. Correction, *I* was going to stage a proposal in the food court during lunch at a mall in Dallas. Crazy, right? Oh, buddy, just get ready.

My team was going around the food court, letting every table know there was about to be a proposal. People were getting off their phones to be ready to record it all. You could feel the anticipation in the air. It was more like Valentine's Day than a random January afternoon.

"Who will he be proposing to?"

That was the problem. My team could only say who was doing the proposing; they couldn't tell them who I was proposing to. And they couldn't tell them because I was scouting out the food court, looking for the lucky gal. I was going to propose to a complete stranger. Do it for the story.

My only criteria was to avoid someone with a ring. It would be awkward for a husband to watch his wife receive a proposal while they were in the Chipotle line. Awkward for him. Unfortunate for me, I'm sure.

Finally, I located a likely candidate. She was in for the biggest surprise of her life.

It started like every good marriage proposal.

"Before I met this girl, I didn't believe in love, but she turned this cold heart into a beating one again." Blah blah blah. Sappy and romantic, but I had to make it believable. I had everyone's attention. Hundreds of people were on the edge of their seat.

"So, people of North Park Mall, join me in asking . . . Jessica"—I threw out a random name—"to marry me."

I turned around and locked eyes with this complete stranger for the first time as I went down to a knee.

Jessica's response was perfect. She was so surprised. She never saw it coming. That's every girl's dream, right? Jessica looked at her friend, looked at me, then looked back at her friend.

"Did he just ask me to marry him? Did you just ask me to marry you?"

It's not every day you get proposed to, and she, completely overwhelmed, buried her head in her arms.

Meanwhile, the food court was going absolutely insane. It had all the characteristics of an actual proposal. She was surprised, overwhelmed, filled with emotion, and utterly embarrassed.

"Aw, look," someone said, "she doesn't know what to do with herself."

What they didn't know was she truly didn't know what to do with herself. It felt as if her head was buried for an eternity, but I wasn't leaving without an answer.

Finally, Jessica lifted her head and said something that, to this day, I will never forget.

"This is the weirdest thing that's ever happened to me," she whispered.

I smiled. I knew what she meant. I stood up to address the crowd, the anticipation was killing them. How do I break the news to the crowd?

"She said yes!"

The building shook.

Jessica was a trooper. I definitely deserved to be slapped. But before I could tell my new fiancée that this was all a joke, a bawling woman approached us. I mean tears flying out of her eyes. She told us she was having a rough day and this just made her day. She took our picture.

"How long have you guys been dating?" she asked.

Jessica put her arm around me and said, "Two and a half years."

I knew I had picked a winner.

I obviously wasn't asking this girl to legitimately marry me, but in the same breath we date a lot like this in the church today. No, we don't ask random people to marry us, but I have seen people get married who didn't really love each other. They didn't marry for the loving union (Gen. 2:24) or the beautiful picture of the gospel that marriage was designed to be (Eph. 5:25). They married because he was single, she was single, and they were each other's ticket out of singleness. How sad is that? They didn't just go on a date, but they got married. Maybe this is one of the reasons why the divorce rate in the church is higher than 50 percent.

Recently, I talked with a girl who said she needed some prayer for direction in her relationship. She said she didn't love him and didn't know what to do. She needed my guidance.

All of my red flags were up and my "get the heck out of here" sirens were going off. I was trying to find the right words to say something in the right way and with the right tone. You know the politically correct way to say, "Simple. Break up with him." I tried, but to me there was no other way to say it. It was like I just told her to torture an animal. "In the Arms of an Angel" started playing in the background. She was appalled and tears filled her eyes.

"But we've been dating for over a year, and I have spent so much time investing in this relationship. I don't want to give up too soon."

Translation: "I'm a twenty-two-year-old senior, and if I don't marry him, I may be alone for the rest of my life. My clock is ticking. I don't want to be like you, Ben, still single at twenty-five. Oh, man, can you imagine?"

We have a problem, and it goes way deeper than just a problem with perspective. The way we view singleness isn't just affecting the way we view a relationship status, but it devalues single people, empowers passivity, robs the church of one of

God's greatest gifts, forces idol worship, and sets up countless marriages for failure. The church is in danger.

Elevation of Marriage Equals Devaluation of Singleness

Our worldview doesn't just devalue a relationship status, it devalues a group of people. The single people in our churches feel less than, not valued, unwanted, waiting for their life to begin. Waiting for a life to begin that began when Jesus died and was raised to life.

We truly believe we can *only* find love and belonging in the arms of a spouse while we completely ignore the people and companionship that has been made so easily available for us now. We treat it like a curse. Like a death sentence. Death by singleness.

We're always looking for our future spouse, waiting for people to set us up left and right. We wake up every day on a mission to find that person who is going to "fix" our singleness problem. Why do we do this? We do this because, since the moment we were born, marriage has been pushed on us as a necessity. A checklist item. Be born, go to school, meet your person, stick to the script.

Sometimes this pressure is applied purposefully. There is a Christian college in the town where I pastor, and some of the things I've heard from these students is absolutely horrifying. Parents send their kids to school and tell them this is where they *will* meet their future spouse. Not that this is the place where they will grow. Not that this is the place where, oh, I don't know, maybe they'll learn since it's *school*. No, but their life is about to begin. Anyone else gag a little? Talk about pressure. No wonder I have people telling me that they will marry their boyfriend even if they don't love them when they become a senior in college. Time is running out. Expectations won't be met.

But I would say, most of the time, this pressure is being applied and people don't even know they're applying it. Some parents apply it purposefully, but some do it and don't even realize they are. *God, I want to pray for Ed's future spouse*, and then they list all the qualities they want in their kid's future spouse. That's great! I'm not saying we need to stop praying for our kid's future marriage. I love that we pray for that, keep praying for that, but we have to change the language of it. *God, if marriage is something you have for my special little sunshine, this is what I pray their spouse would look like.* Yes, I said *if.* Marriage is not a promise of God. Nowhere in Scripture does God promise us marriage. *We need to stop writing checks God doesn't always intend to cash.*

Imagine what would happen if parents in the church prayed for God to use their kid in their season of singleness to wreak havoc for his kingdom? Man, think of the empowerment that would provide! Instead of throwing false promises and expectations of what their life is supposed to look like, or at least what they expect their life to look like, they are empowering them to feel like they can do something now. Maybe that's why we have such a passive church these days. Everyone thinks that once you live out the American dream—get a spouse, kids, and a nice house—that's when life begins. But from knowing many people who are in that life stage, the common theme I see is that they are stretched incredibly thin, not to mention exhausted. They have all they want, but the effect they thought they would have isn't there.

Simple misplacement of cause and effect. I'll get married (cause), and then I'll start living the kingdom life (effect). I'll preach the gospel, lead my family, and get in community because now I have the support system I've been longing for. They get married (cause), but they rarely do the effect. Their time has been cut off at the knees. They realize the time in their life when they could've done the effect most effectively was actually in their singleness. Back then there was no one they had to devote themselves to, no one who was completely dependent on them. But that season is long gone now, in their rearview mirror. They were God's gift to the church, but since they never felt empowered or encouraged, that gift was left unwrapped and drastically misused.

Here's the problem with our perspective on singleness. We force ourselves to live in a constant hypothetical world. When we're single, we think we'll start the kingdom life when we're married. If we get married, we wish we would've done the kingdom life when we had the time in our singleness. The problem: kingdom life becomes hypothetical and never gets done. The vision for the church Jesus had when he left is tabled and the "greater things" promised in John 14 never happen. It's not just a perspective problem; it becomes a failure to live out our purpose. A purpose we don't believe exists in our singleness.

Silence Also Communicates and Robs the Church

The pressure is not always felt with what people say, but a lot of the time it's felt in what people don't say. A church that goes to work is God's church. Plain and simple. The church should be empowering and equipping people to go out and use their gifts to build up the body of Christ (Eph. 4:12). The church shouldn't be a one- or two-man show, but instead should be a bunch of members functioning in different roles as one body (1 Cor. 12:12, 14, 27).

One of the biggest gifts God has given the church so they can get to work is single people. They should be the backbone of our church. Our churches should be inundated with serving single people, but for most churches that is nowhere near the case. Two tragic things are happening: (1) single people aren't using their gifts and (2) churches aren't utilizing their gift of single people. Churches aren't efficiently going to work.

And here's the crazy part, after I spoke on singleness at my church, the most common thing I heard from people was that they had never heard of singleness as a gift before that morning. I was the first pastor they heard who talked about singleness as a gift, *and* I was the first pastor they heard who talked about singleness, period. If single people are the people who can most effectively use their gifts for God's kingdom, shouldn't the church be entering into this conversation at least semiregularly? Why do we treat singleness as a taboo subject? We're afraid to enter into this conversation for some reason. Let me tell you from personal experience, singleness isn't contagious. Just because you talk about singleness as a gift, God isn't going to go, "Oh, you think it's a gift? If you love singleness so much, here you go!" By treating singleness as taboo, do you know what you communicate? Single people are taboo.

I was a finance and economics major in college, which meant I did a lot of math. One day we had a test in a class that required a financial calculator, and my buddy showed up with a regular calculator. That would never work. It would be like trying to ride a bike up a mountain with no wheels. You can pedal really fast, but it won't do the job. I could've just sat there and let my friend try and take that test with that calculator, but that would've made me a terrible friend and incredibly unloving. I didn't want to see him fail, so I lovingly communicated with him in time for him to make the necessary adjustments.

Does that mean the church has been incredibly unloving toward single people? By not empowering single people, the church is wasting the gift God has given them and not being good stewards of the resources God has blessed them with (1 Cor. 4:2).

I'm not saying we need to be doing a monthlong sermon series about singleness, but I am saying this is not a topic we can afford to ignore. It needs to be talked about, and it needs to be talked about in the right way. Single people need to be encouraged and empowered, not pushed to find a spouse. If they find a person and get married, then that's amazing. I'm not saying we need to encourage single people to avoid marriage, but we need to encourage them not to run from singleness. And whether we want to believe it or not, if we don't enter into these conversations but choose to stay silent, then single people will continue to stay on the sideline.

When we don't speak up about something, knowingly or unknowingly, it insinuates that we agree with what is being said. If someone introduces you by the wrong name, what are you going to do? Stay silent or correct it? Ninety-nine percent of people would correct the person who called them by the wrong name. *Silence isn't staying out of the conversation; silence is raucously reinforcing the loudest voices.*

By staying silent, we are loudly communicating to single people that their life hasn't begun. Why would they want to serve the church and use their gifts when they don't feel complete or empowered? They're spending their time trying to find their fulfillment in a person instead of finding fulfillment in their purpose.

One day we, as leaders in the church, will stand before God and give an account of how we stewarded the resources he gave us. We have countless meetings throughout the year to discuss how we should handle the finances of the church. How will we respond when God asks us how we loved and empowered his wonderful gift of single people? Will we be a church that goes to work or a church that stays on the sideline?

Misplaced Worship

A few months ago, I had a relationship not work out. If you would've asked me before the relationship if marriage was an idol in my life, I would've emphatically said no. I mean, after all, I preached a sermon on singleness. I should have it all figured out, right?

I desired marriage at a very unhealthy level. It was so hard to see. My community asked me, before the relationship, if it didn't work out if I would be okay, and I said I would be fine. After the first date I realized how wrong I was. I wanted it so badly that, if it didn't work out, I would be devastated.

Ever wonder why we make relationships a big deal, bigger than the relationship warrants? Why that's the rule instead of the exception? Get ready. Buckle your seat belt. It's about to get bumpy and convicting. We make relationships a big deal because our savior, our idol has now put on flesh. We go from worshiping an idea to worshiping a person. Our idea of marriage is imaginary, but a person is tangible.

Eventually devastation set in when the relationship didn't work out. I was angry. I was confused. I was frustrated. Some days I didn't even want to get out of bed. My meaning and purpose were temporarily nonexistent. I had to come face-to-face with the reality that I had been worshiping marriage. I put marriage on the throne that only Jesus can sit on. How did I come to that conclusion? How did I know marriage and the girl I was pursuing had become an idol?

We cling to what we worship when times get tough. When we worship something, we put a lot of trust and hope in that thing, so when times get tough, we run to what we worship for comfort and safety. When Jonah was on the boat, fleeing from God, and a dangerous storm came, all of the mariners "each cried out to his god" (Jonah 1:5) to save them. Well, when the storms of life come, we do the same things those sailors did in the book of Jonah: we cry out to our gods. We cry out to what we worship.

This is why God tells us to have no other gods before him (Ex. 20:3). God is a God of order (1 Cor. 14:33). He is not someone whose commandments are burdensome (1 John 5:3). When the seas get rough, we reach for the thing we worship most to keep our heads above water. We search for that steady, unwavering, immovable force in a sea of instability and confusion. And when we hold on to anything other than God, we drown.

The relationship ended and my life buoy went with it. It led to complete devastation. I felt susceptible on the open waters. I was holding on to something and thinking it would keep me afloat, but I was drowning. One of my mentors told me that sadness is a part of life, but devastation only occurs when an idol is taken away. Even though this really hurt, this was the grace of God in my life to point out an idol that was in my blind spot. So many people enter into marriage and have no idea they aren't worshiping God but worshiping their future spouse. They put all their hope and trust in their marriage, and when the seas get rough, they try to hold on to something that will surely cause them to sink.

We have more than just a perspective problem. The way we view singleness is robbing us of all of our purpose now. We've been given a gift and have been made as a gift for the body of Christ, but it is drastically being misused. In most cases it's not being used at all. We are robbing ourselves, and the church is reinforcing that idea with their words or lack of words. Marriage is a gift, not a god.

Single people, we have an incredible purpose now, but if nothing changes, we're in incredible danger of never fully living it out. And that should scare us.

Chapter 3

Loving but Damaging Advice

Have you ever witnessed anybody give advice that was totally wrong? You try to hide the confused look on your face, but it's impossible due to the foolishness of what you just heard? When I was in high school, I was on the basketball team. We only had one court to practice on, so the varsity guys would practice after the girls and the JV were done practicing. Most guys on the varsity team would go to McDonald's to flirt with diabetes, but I stayed after school to watch the two teams practice and finish my homework. (I know, nerd alert.)

I walked into the locker room one day and ran into a frazzled JV head coach. He seemed relieved to see me, as he said, "Oh, thank God, it's you." He told me that an emergency had come up, so he left one of the parents to run practice. He pretty much begged me to run practice until he returned. I was confused but agreed. I walked into the gym and quickly realized why he was so relieved to see me. It was obvious the parent had absolutely no idea what he was doing. Obvious.

They were doing lay-ups lines, but practice was stopped and the parent was intensely coaching the boys on the "correct" way to do lay-ups. It wasn't the right way at all. He was telling them to jump off the wrong foot. The team looked confused, considering they learned this fundamental at the age of five, and they looked to me for help. I told the parent I was taking over practice and hoped deep down inside that the boys didn't listen to his coaching.

But some of them listened. I mean, an adult told them they were doing it wrong, so they must be doing it wrong.

I quietly informed the team they were doing lay-ups the right way before. Situation over, right? Wrong. After each kid did their lay-up, a voice boomed from the bleachers, "Wrong foot!" The parent didn't leave. He stayed to watch practice, and now he was back-seat, bleacher-sitting coaching. I was sixteen years old; he was forty plus. They don't teach you how to navigate this situation in chemistry class.

I told the boys to ignore him, including his own son. Awkward does not even begin to describe the situation. Once the head coach came back, I ended up going into the bleachers to inform this parent about the correct way to do a lay-up. It was so weird, but I couldn't stand idly by as I watched the team be fed flat-out wrong information. His intentions weren't bad. He thought he was giving accurate advice. But if the team took his advice, they would look ridiculous attempting lay-ups and would not have much success in making them.

This very situation is happening with single people today. Singleness can be hard. Correction, singleness *is* hard at times. And people lovingly walk alongside single people and give them advice. Unfortunately, most of the time they're more like this dad trying to coach high schoolers how to attempt lay-ups. Their intentions are pure, but the advice, a lot of times, is damaging and flat-out not biblical.

I've mentioned this before, but singleness has been a really tough pill to swallow lately. I have a roommate whom I spend most of my free time with who is also single. When I didn't have a plan for a Friday or Saturday night, he was the friend I knew I would be hanging out with on those nights. Romantic, right? He was my number-one choice, and I was his. We perfected picking up Chili's to-go and watching movies on Netflix. No one did it better. Recently, however, my roommate boldly moved into the dating world. My dude, my ride-or-die, found a new Chili's-to-go, Netflix-watching person.

There isn't anyone in the world who has been more excited for him about this. Seriously, I mean that. But I'm really sad for me. Instead of spending my Friday nights with him, I'm spending them predominantly by myself. I now don't know what I'm doing on the weekend and don't know who I'm doing it with. That has been really hard.

I'm not proud to say I've thrown some pity parties and, not surprisingly, I was the only one who showed up. It's been difficult. I'm surrounded by so many amazing people. I feel so loved. But at the same time, right now, I don't feel wanted. For the first time in my life, I'm nobody's number one.

These feelings and situations are very common for single people. In the tough seasons, we need people to encourage us and point us back to the truth. People to love us enough to help lift the veil and reveal what the reality of the situation is. In singleness sometimes the advice that is given comes from a great place, but it isn't helpful in revealing truth. Sometimes it does the opposite, it does more damage than good, and it is flat-out wrong.

In this chapter we're going to shed some light on what common advice is communicated to single people. The goal of this isn't to guilt, the goal is to reveal advice that either isn't helpful or just flat-out wrong.

There's a way to lovingly give single people advice, but there is some advice we need to stop giving.

"Just Be Patient; They're Coming"

This is by far the most common advice I give my single friends. Most of the time bad advice can sound like good advice because it has some truth sprinkled on top. When you tell someone to be patient, it sounds biblical. Patience is a fruit of the Spirit (Gal. 5:22), God tells us to be patient in tribulation (Rom. 12:12), and love is patient (1 Cor. 13:4). If love is patient, then I'll wait patiently for it.

Yes, we need to be patient, but then I ask, "Be patient for what?" Be patient and wait for the Lord, his timing, and his will because he is good? Or be patient and wait for a spouse? God has a plan today that is deeper than any earthly relationship. Waiting sounds so passive. We need to wait for the Lord to establish our steps (Prov. 16:9), but waiting doesn't mean sitting on the sideline.

Waiting also implies that something is coming. What if we're telling people to be patient and wait for something that God doesn't have for them? Imagine this for a second. I have a lot of friends who have younger kids, and one of the most common things I hear kids whine to their parents about is their hunger.

"Mom, when is dinner?" *Wait for it.* "I'm starving!"

Mom usually gives a "be patient, dinner is coming soon to a table near you" statement. What if the mom said that and dinner never came? Ever? After a few days, the starving child is now wondering how good her mom really is, because she said it was coming, and she hasn't delivered on her promise.

Why do we throw expectations onto people and call them promises of God when God never promises those things? Do I believe most people reading this book will end up married? Yes, I do, but that doesn't make it a certainty. When we say, "Be patient, they're coming," my questions are, "What if they aren't?" "What if God's plan for their life is to remain single?"

As a single person, that is a truly terrifying thought. Single forever? What kind of sick person would want someone to endure that? But if this was the case for my life (as it will be for some people), I would have just as much meaning as the people who will get married.

When the people who have been given that advice for years get older, and they are still with no prospect in sight, it leads to some major frustration with God. "Wow, I guess all my friends are being taken care of, and I'm forgotten and just shoved into a corner. Thanks, God." They wonder why they're not married yet, when this is something people have told them their whole lives is a promise of God. A certainty.

We can make promises to things that are certainties. Of course, a mom is going to feed her kids. They need it to survive. God will supply us all the things we need (Matt. 6:32–33). We need food, but we don't need marriage.

"You Just Have To _____"

As an overthinker, I drive all of my mentors crazy with how much I overthink things. Especially in relationships. In high school I sat up front with my coach on away trips and asked him a thousand questions while he drove the bus.

"At the end of this text message she put two periods instead of one. Do you think she meant, 'Have a good night dot dot dot?' Oh, man, do you think she's about to breakup with me?"

It would drive my coach insane.

"No, Ben, she probably just accidentally hit an extra period and is literally not thinking about breaking up with you at all." (Get ready for the line that everyone uses on me.) "Get out of your own head."

I've been given this advice before in many different ways. "You just have to be more aggressive." (That's biblical, like Ruth and Boaz and like Jacob and Rachel).

"You just have to play the game." (Which I have played and I think is stupid. More on that later).

I mean, fill in the blank with whatever you've heard.

When I have been the recipient of this advice, it gets into my head. I try and find ways to manipulate situations to get a girl to notice me or go out with me. I think I'm in control. Emphasis on *think*.

How awful is that? I turn what should be the enjoyable, natural experience of meeting someone into a stress-filled, overthought manipulation. But I'm not just manipulating a situation, because I end up fantasizing about manipulating another person.

"I'll say hi, ask her how she's doing, then say I have to go, leaving her wanting more because I need to 'stop being so aggressive.'"

It's not the best advice. It can easily communicate if you just wore this, said this, or did that, then you would be married by now. If you were just worthy enough, you wouldn't still be single.

What if you're single, not because you're not doing enough or doing too much, but because God wants you to be single? I'll rephrase that. No matter how hard singleness is, if we believe God is sovereign and in control, then we are single because God wants us to be. He willed us to be. What if we've done everything right, but God just didn't open their eyes?

There are times when this advice is 100 percent needed, though. Passivity is a growing characteristic in the next generation, especially in men. Sometimes guys won't ask out girls because they're afraid of rejection. There have been times when I was afraid to ask someone out because I wasn't sure if they liked me back. I wished I was back in junior high, where I could ask their bestie if they liked me, and they could give me the thumbs up or down. The world doesn't work that way anymore, at least not in the circles I run in. It's a risk. They could say no. Sometimes we need to be told, "Just put yourself out there."

"They're Just Intimidated by You"

I might need you to hold my beverage for this one.

In the conversations I've had, this advice is most common for women to hear. I have some very strong opinions on this advice, and, yes, I will share them, but this advice has confused the people I've talked to way more than its helped. *They feel like they can't be themselves, because if nothing changes, neither will their relationship status.*

"You just have to tone it down," I was once told during a job interview. They told me I had a lot of energy, but it could come off as fake. They wanted me to tone it down. I believe God has blessed me and gifted me with a lot of energy. This gift has allowed me to connect with people more quickly than if I had less energy. The advisers recommended I take it down to about

80 percent when I first met people. I left the job interview not feeling understood. It felt as if they would only hire me if I would change who I was. Instead of being told to embrace my gifts, I was told to be somebody I was not. I didn't feel empowered. I felt ashamed.

Many girls have told me this is the same advice they receive from their friends and family. It stings. It brings me back to that job interview. "People will only like me if I'm not myself."

If someone doesn't like you for who you are, then they aren't the person for you. Don't try to be somebody different. Girls, some guys are intimidated by a confident woman with a big personality, but this has nothing to do with you and has everything to do with their own insecurities. They are intimidated because you are often more confident and surer of yourself than they are.

We should be searching for people who love us for who we are. Anyone who wants us to change who we are just isn't the one for us. I hope you understand I'm not giving anyone an excuse for sin. If someone sees sin in your life, and they call it out, you shouldn't say, "You just need to love me for who I am. I'm not changing for anyone." If anyone you're dating says that to you, *run!*

"Stop Being So Picky"

This is the most common advice I receive from people. I'm not somebody who will just go on a date to get to know someone, so the time between one date and the next is pretty significant usually. There have been a few people my friends have tried to set me up with that I have respectfully turned down.

"You just have unrealistic expectations."

"You're too shallow."

Maybe, and if that's the case and I'm loving things in the opposite sex that God doesn't love, then my community needs to call me out. But what if people aren't too picky? What if they just know who they're looking for? What if they aren't willing to settle? What if they want to be a good leader and brother or sister in Christ and don't want to play with anyone's heart when they know it won't work out?

"You're getting older, a lot of the catches are already taken. Time to lower your standards." Is marriage such a necessity that we need to lower our standards because the top prospects have all made it to the big leagues? Does God become less sovereign the longer we're single?

"It Happens When You Least Expect It"

My high school girlfriend and I had just broken up, and I was down and out. I ended up going to a married friend's home to process the breakup, and I received possibly the weirdest advice I have ever encountered.

"Ben, I knew this relationship was doomed to fail because you were anticipating this relationship for a long time," he said. "Stuff like this happens when you least expect it."

He then went into how he met his wife, but I didn't hear a word of it, because I was trying to wrap my mind around the insanity of what he had just said. I bet the story had something to do with meeting his wife and not expecting it at all. I'd put money on it. Also, ready for some irony? They're now divorced.

So, let me get this straight, the reason I don't have a wife is because I desire to have one? I have to get to the point where I don't desire one, and then God will give me one? I'm sorry, this advice is really hard for me to process. There's no logic behind it, and not an ounce of biblical support.

But it's very common advice to hear in singleness. I say "in singleness" because no one gives this advice *in any other situation.*

"You'll be healed of cancer only when you least expect it."

"You'll get that job promotion when you least expect it."

"You'll have kids when you least expect it."

"You haven't had kids yet because you want it too much."

You don't hear it, and you never will. This advice communicates that a longing or a desire for a relationship is bad, and the Lord won't bring it unless you're not looking for it or focused on it. This isn't backed up by Scripture, in fact, it opposes it. "If you then, who are evil, know how to give good gifts to your children, how much more will your Father who is in heaven give good things to those who ask him!" (Matt. 7:11). It's okay for us to desire a relationship, but don't let it rule your life and become ultimate. And remember, marriage is good too.

"You Just Haven't Found the Right One Yet"

Dang, what gave it away?

"Once Your Eyes Are Completely Focused on the Lord, Then They'll Come"

Can this be the case? Can somebody have marriage in their future as God's plan for them, but God's waiting because this hypothetical someone isn't in the place they need to be for marriage? Yes, I truly believe this could be the case. Is this always the case though? Absolutely not. Not all single people aren't ready for marriage. Also, who has ever been *ready* for marriage? Has anyone ever walked into marriage and was amazing at it? Never made a mistake? Never needed to learn anything from failing?

This advice is the one that inspired me to write this book. There are countless articles that talk about singleness from a biblical perspective, and many of them say this very thing. "God doesn't give blessings to people when they're not ready to receive them. We receive blessings in our spiritual bucket, and if it has any holes in it, why would God try and fill this bucket?" A lot of people, including myself, believe this advice. "Am I missing something, God? Do I not love you enough to be blessed with companionship and a spouse?"

It also leads people to believe God works only on a carrot-and-stick system. When I am performing for God, and he is pleased with me, then he'll reward me. When I'm not where I need to be and not living for him, then he'll take things away or withhold things that are good.

That's not how God works. This completely eliminates his mercy and grace.

What have we ever done that caused us to deserve anything good from God? We don't deserve his grace, mercy, love, or life that he gives us (Eph. 2:8–9; Titus 3:5; Rom. 6:23, 5:8). We were dead in our sins and trespasses, but he came in human flesh to die for our sins, taking the punishment and wrath we deserved, all because of *his* mercy and despite our own sin. If God did only work on the carrot-and-stick system, then we would never receive any blessings from him and would be spending eternity in hell.

This advice, though it makes some kind of sense, cannot be more opposite to the gospel.

"I Don't Know How You're Still Single"

This may be the advice that's given with the greatest heart behind it. The person who says this usually sees how amazing their single friend is and is confused how other people don't see what they see. Great, loving intentions. And the times when people have said this to me, it makes me feel so loved, but it also leads to some bitterness and frustration. Especially in unhealthy seasons, this advice can communicate one of two things.

The first frustration is with all the women out there who have broken my heart or have told me no. "Yeah, you're right. I am amazing. They just couldn't see it." But at the end of the day, it didn't work out because it wasn't part of God's will. Plain and simple. I believe God opens and closes our eyes to each other. It's not because they couldn't see the beautiful gem that we singles are (or I *think* I am), it's because God is sovereign and didn't make it happen.

The second frustration is with the person offering this advice. "If I'm such a catch, then why is nothing happening? If I really were as awesome as you say I am, then shouldn't women be lining up by the dozens?"

It's okay to not know how or why you or someone else is "still" single (by saying "still single" you're also implying that one day they'll be married), but just because we don't know something, it doesn't mean there isn't an incredible purpose behind it.

The Gospel and Singleness

Before we get into some of the ways we can encourage our single friends, we have to realize that maybe the best way we can love them is by saying nothing at all. My friends want to vent and feel listened to, but I try to say the most profound thing I can to make it easier for them. It doesn't always work that way, however. It actually very rarely works that way. You don't need to have the answers. Release yourself from that burden.

We need companionship. We need a friend. We don't always need advice or someone to "fix" it.

Sometimes the best thing to do is to listen to your friend, maybe sit with them for a while, pray for them, and then destroy a pint (or maybe a half gallon) of ice cream and watch a movie.

Sidenote: Why is eating ice cream and watching movies only a stereotype for women? I'm always down for a bowl of ice cream and a movie.

"Marriage Isn't the End All Be All"

I love having so many married friends to walk through life with. Many of them have been walking with me while I've really struggled in my singleness, and it's always a positive perspective shift when they tell me marriage isn't the end all be all. A married friend told me some of their loneliest nights have been while they were lying in bed next to their spouse.

It's okay to long for and desire a relationship, but it's also healthy that while God has you there (for however long that may be) to continually surrender this desire to the Lord. It's okay to pray this desire will take the seat in our hearts where it belongs. Not so high where it becomes an idol, not so low where we downplay the gift of marriage. It's also okay to pray over your future spouse if that's what the Lord has for you. It's borderline passive not to.

It's a cliché, but remind your single friends that Jesus and his disciples were single in the Gospel accounts (except Peter, but Peter is usually the exception to most rules anyway). They were completely whole and satisfied and impacted the kingdom in some incredible ways. They didn't need anything because they were walking with Jesus figuratively and literally. *They didn't need anything because they had everything.*

Singleness Reflects the Sufficiency of Christ.

There is always so much talk about how marriage is a great picture of Christ and his love for the church (Eph. 5:25–32), but we don't talk about how singleness is a picture of the sufficiency of Christ.

I have spent multiple Friday nights alone since my roommate started dating. They've been hard and lonely, but I've had people in my corner encouraging me to lean into that loneliness.

We're not alone. We'll never be alone. We have a God who is absolutely crazy about us and will never leave us or forsake us (Deut. 31:8; Heb. 13:5). And when we feel alone and abandoned by people, we have to remind ourselves of the person who never will leave us. And that person is the one who has already won our hearts. God wanted them so desperately he died to get them.

This isn't a comprehensive list of advice we can and should not be giving our single friends, but the goal of this chapter isn't to find the best things to say. Rather, we need to change our mindset. We need to put to death our desire to fix it and make our single friends feel better with our words. Words are necessary sometimes, but what has helped me most when things have been tough in my singleness is when my friends were just there. They invited me over for dinner, and we just laughed and talked about seemingly meaningless things. No advice was given.

My prayer is for us to be less like the parent who flippantly ran basketball practice and more like the friend who was just there when we needed someone to be there.

Chapter 4

Problem with the Giver, Not the Gift

Junior high. Man, what a time to be alive. I work with them every day, and every day I say to myself, "I can't believe that was me."

Recently, one of our junior high girls started liking another boy in the student ministry. All night she was running around, trying to capture enough of his attention to ask him to the junior high prom. It was hilarious to watch while he awkwardly stood there, looking like he'd rather die or just melt into the ground. It ended with both of them crying and the small group leaders attempting to console them. Sounds accurate, doesn't it?

The episode reminded me of one of my first crushes. I was in seventh grade and was head over heels for a girl. I was *sure* she was the one for me. I asked my parents if I could ask her out, expecting them to share my same excitement, considering she was going to be their future daughter-in-law, but I was totally wrong.

They told me I wasn't allowed to date, so asking her out was out of the question. I didn't feel understood. I was frustrated and probably said something like, "You just don't want me to be happy." Which was met with, "How did you know that was our mission? We thought we were being sneaky about it. Time to change our game plan."

They explained how dating at my age was pointless and was inevitably going to end in heartbreak. They were trying to protect me from the distress and drama that accompanies junior high relationships. But I saw it a lot differently. I was in love. How could they not see it? I walked by her in the hallway the other day and almost passed out. That's love, right?

They may have said no, but nothing can stop love or me for that matter when I have my mind set on something. The next day I did what any junior high kid does when they're in love. I asked her best friend if she liked me. I got the green light and was going to slip the "check yes or no" note in her locker later. Asking her out in person would be too risky, and, honestly, the idea of talking to her made me want to throw up.

Well, that idea got hijacked real quick. Her best friend, who was way bigger than me, told me I needed to ask her out during the next class period. I told her my plan, but she disapproved and told me it was now or never. I chose never. I didn't like her that much anyways. That was the end of it, right? Nope. After the most painful nipple pinching I've ever experienced, I reluctantly agreed to ask her out. When I walked into history class, I could tell by the look on my love's face that she had been pressured as well. Just a modern-day Romeo and Juliet.

I was on the opposite side of the classroom and looked at her. She looked at me. This is the moment. Make or break. What came out of my mouth next would dictate our future together. This would be the story we would tell our children.

"So? You wanna go out or what?"

Okay, not the best delivery, I'll give you that.

She answered, "No." And it wasn't an "Oh, I'm so flattered, but no thank you, maybe next time." There was no hesitation at all. In fact, there was more disgust than anything else.

And the class erupted in laughter. It was so shocking and hilarious, even the teacher was laughing.

Our fairy-tale ended before it could even begin.

It's funny and I can joke about it now, because it was just a silly junior high relationship. I look back and laugh and think how ridiculous all of it was. Of course, life would move on if I didn't date her, but at the time I thought my life was over and was incredibly frustrated with my parents. If they would've allowed me to date her, I wouldn't have been forced to hide it, and they could've even helped me find a cool way to ask her out. How could they not see this was what was best for me?

But they were right all along. (I'm sure they're going to love reading those words.) They could see how this would end, and they could not only see this relationship wasn't what was best for me, they saw it would lead down a very dark road. Their saying no was the most loving thing they could do.

That was the seventh grade. I've grown up a lot since then, but I still play this same game with God. There are things in life that I just *know* are best for me, and when he doesn't give those things to me, I question his goodness. I question his motives as if he's on a mission to ruin my life. How could he not see this was what was best for me?

I do this most with singleness. There are countless sermons and articles that tell us singleness is a gift, and the reason we don't see it as a gift is because we have a perspective problem. If we just viewed singleness the way God did, then we would be pumped about it.

I don't believe this is the root of the problem. *If we spent less time focusing on the gift and trying to understand why and spent more time focusing on the giver of the gift, I believe our perspective would begin to shift.* This is where I have struggled. I have tried to put God in a box to better understand him, so I can try and see why he has given me this very odd gift. But that hasn't helped because when I compare the blessings of singleness to the blessings of marriage, it doesn't make sense as to why a loving God would actively choose to give his children singleness.

The Bible, however, paints a different picture. It tells us to trust in the Lord with all of our hearts and *not* to trust our own understanding (Prov. 3:5). When the Lord gives us a gift and we don't understand it, we're not always called to understand why. God is infinite. We are finite. No one can understand God (Job 36:26). His thoughts are not our thoughts, and his ways are not our ways (Isa. 55:8–9). There may be times God will give us gifts that don't make any sense to us. But what if we took our focus off of the gifts and turned our focus on the giver of the gifts and his character?

The Sin of Control

I have struggled with control for a long time. I want to be in control, and if I can't be in control, then I think whatever I'm doing is doomed to fail. Obviously. The last few months have been some of the hardest I've ever had to go through. I have felt so out of control. It has scared me and caused me some serious sadness and crippling anxiety.

My desire to control is sin. Just flat-out not trusting God. For some reason, I believe I'm more reliable than God and my future is better in my hands than in the hands of the God of the universe. As I told you earlier, a breakup led me to write this book. It devastated me. I had an idea of what I wanted my life to look like, and God very quickly ripped it from my hands. Hands that were closed and holding on tightly to what I wanted.

Now that I look back, I can see there were multiple times God was calling me to let go, but my pride and my selfish ambition wouldn't allow me to. So, when all my plans were ripped from my hands, it hurt. It hurt way more than if I would've just let God lead. I wish that would've been the lesson learned. I wish I would've taken the hint. "Okay, God, you're in control. I give up." Sadly, I was way too stubborn.

I ended up pigheadedly getting back into a relationship with the girl who originally broke my heart. No one in my community thought it was a good idea, but I did what I wanted because apparently, I like to learn things the hard way. Well, that relationship ended the same way. Heartbreak and I were reintroduced.

I was hurt and felt like I did after the girl in seventh grade told me no. I thought the same things. "God, why don't you want me to be happy? Obviously, this is what's best for me, and you took it away."

I wrestled with that for months, which made the suffering even more intense. Not only was I dealing with heartbreak, but I was fighting with God. And here's the crazy thing: God was humble enough to take it.

One day I was talking to a mentor, and he was calling me out for some areas of my life that weren't looking like Jesus. It was a big moment. I realized I wasn't looking like Jesus because I wasn't walking with him. And I couldn't faithfully walk with God, because I was trying to be him. I needed either to surrender all of my life (my future and my relationships) or to surrender none of it.

We were created to be dependent on God. There are many times God brings us into situations that are obviously out of our control. God was sharpening me. He loved me, but he loved me too much to let me stay where I was. I realized during this season that the more I allowed God to lead, the more alive and at peace I felt.

How is this possible? When we let go of control, we're not letting go of the reins and letting God lead, we're letting go of the *idea* that we had the reins in the first place. We aren't in control. And here's the thing: we never have been.

The other day I was hanging out with a friend. We were driving around, looking for a place to eat, and I was in the back seat with his two-year-old son. There was a little play steering wheel in the back, and whenever the car turned right, his little boy would turn his toy steering wheel to the right. I laughed until I cried. This kid legitimately thought he was driving the car. He wouldn't even look at me. He had to keep his eyes on the road.

Isn't this what we're trying to do with God? God has always been driving the car, and we have always been in the back seat in our car seat, gripping a steering wheel and thinking we are the ones driving. Sometimes we turn the wheel right, and the car turns right. God is good. He answers the prayers of his children, but the car turns right because *he* directed it that way.

Then there are times we turn the wheel to the right, but the blessings of God and his will take us left. We pitch a fit. "This isn't what I want! Really? Why didn't that relationship work out? How am I still single? I've tried to get off the last six exits, but *nope*, guess that's not good enough for God!"

When we let go of control, we acknowledge we are cute little kids sitting in the back and holding a fake steering wheel and the God of the universe—who loves us so much he didn't spare his own son, but gave him up for us (Rom. 8:32)—has our best interests in mind (Rom. 8:28), rewards those who seek him (Heb. 11:6), and is the one ultimately guiding the ship. Or in this case, the car.

We have a father-son relationship with him, and in that relationship, we have so much security when we come to terms with what is really going on. He is in control, and he is trustworthy with it. This relationship brings security and peace, but it also means we don't have as much control as we want. Sometimes Father says no. And that's okay.

"If you then, who are evil, know how to give good gifts to your children, how much more will your Father who is in heaven give good things to those who ask him!" (Matt. 7:11). *Good things. Not always the things we want.* We don't "struggle" with control. We are either trusting God or we are sinning by trying to be him.

Trust Isn't Easy

"God is in control."

"Let go and let God."

We hear those phrases so much it doesn't really have an effect when we hear it. We know it, but just because we know something doesn't make it easy to live out. I can talk about control as if I have it figured out. But that would be the furthest thing from the truth. Yes, there are moments I trust the Lord with my life, and then five seconds later I'm back to having my next "my life is over" mini-panic attack.

We don't always have to be 100 percent confident in the Lord to trust him. Okay, that's a shocking statement, but bear with me. Obviously, that is the ideal. We want to fully trust the Lord, but there's something so beautiful about trusting someone when logic tells us not to.

Have you ever done a trust fall? You stand on a raised platform and fall blindly toward some people with the expectation they will catch you. I don't care who you are or who those people are, there is going to be some fear. Even if you trust them completely, you're thinking, *What if they drop me?* It doesn't take 100 percent trust to have your feet leave the platform. It just takes 51 percent. Trust isn't always saying you know for a fact you will be caught, but your belief that you will be caught overpowers your belief that you'll be dropped. "Faith is not the absence of doubt; it is continuing to follow Jesus in the midst of doubt" (J. D. Greear).

If God really is good, and if he is a Father who is truly all powerful and fully in control, then whatever we have been given must be what's best for us. "For the Lord God is a sun and shield; the Lord bestows favor and honor. No good thing does he withhold from those who walk uprightly" (Ps. 84:11). I can hear it and believe it, but when I come home after a long day and want to decompress with someone I love, I can promise you, I'm not 100 percent trusting in Psalm 84:11. But I have a choice at that moment: does my trust in the Lord overpower my desire to be married?

Do we trust the giver of the gift even when we can't see how this can be what's best for us?

Growing up, my family had season passes to Busch Gardens in Tampa, Florida. The first few years of my life, going to Busch Gardens had to be incredibly boring for my parents. I was too small to ride any of the rides, so we just walked around and looked at the animals. It's five million degrees outside, no breeze, and we went around to watch animals lay in the sun. But one summer my dad measured me before we left, and I was finally tall enough to ride the roller coaster known as the Scorpion.

We arrived at the park and made a beeline for the roller coaster. My dad couldn't contain his excitement. The animal-watching days were over. We got to the ride, and in a split second I realized I didn't want to ride it. But my dad didn't give me a choice.

"You have to ride it at least one time, and if you don't like it, you never have to ride it ever again."

As you can imagine, that wasn't comforting to me at all. The coaster went upside down. There would be no next time when my little four-year-old self fell out.

The line was short, and we got to the front in record time. The guy on the PA was talking about feeling "the sting of the scorpion." That really didn't help. When it was our turn to take a seat on the ride, I started screaming at the top of my lungs, "No, I don't want to."

Everyone was looking at us. I mean, even at four, I loved drama. But people were also staring because my loving, sympathetic father was laughing. He was laughing so hard his face was red.

He picked me up, put me in the coaster next to him, and strapped me in. I never stopped screaming. He never stopped laughing. And no one there was rushing up to give him the Father of the Year award.

The coaster took off and we began the upward ascent toward my death. The ride couldn't have lasted more than forty seconds. We returned to the station. My dad was still laughing, but the difference was: so was I. I looked to the 1999 Father of the Year and said, "Let's go again!"

Today I am a huge roller coaster enthusiast. There isn't a roller coaster I won't ride, but I had to be put in a situation that was uncomfortable by someone who loved me to show me that. And do you want to know something beautiful? The person who put me in the coaster, sat right next to me the whole time.

God allows us to go through uncomfortable situations so that he can bless us. But we have to be careful of our definition of blessing. There are teachings out there that tell us we go through tough times so God can give us the desires of our heart.

"Sacrifice to the Lord, and he will give you that promotion."

"Follow Jesus wholeheartedly, and then you'll get into that relationship you have been longing for."

Yes, it's true that God wants to bless us, but not always with the things we *think* we want. Sometimes he blesses us with suffering. Sometimes he blesses us with sickness. Sometimes he blesses us by saying no to the things we want. Because when we get blessed with those things, we are forced to run to him. We are forced to wake up every day 100 percent dependent on him.

Sometimes he takes away, and that is really hard to comprehend. Very rarely does God ever involve us when he's making decisions for our lives. And we need to thank God that he doesn't. We have no idea what we need. Why? Well, because we're not God, no matter how hard we try to be.

We are always in such a hurry to find answers and to find out when the next thing is coming. But what if God just wants us to sit and be with him and not do anything? What if it's not looking for the next best thing? What if the next best thing is just sitting in his presence and pursuing him, not a relationship? What if the gift isn't marriage, but instead it's falling more in love with our Savior and trusting him even when it doesn't logically make sense?

What if he wants us to sit next to him in the rollercoaster and just enjoy the ride?

Our Understanding Is Flawed

Not knowing the answer to something doesn't mean there isn't an answer. It's a hard reality to not know, but we have to realize that our understanding is incredibly finite. We're trying to understand things that are way above our pay grade.

Our trying to understand God and the infinite nature of his character and will is like a third grader trying to understand the complexities of string theory (to be honest with you, I don't even know what string theory is—it just sounds complex). Just because a third grader doesn't understand it doesn't make the string theorist wrong or inept. It actually does the opposite; it shows the limitations of being a third grader.

We don't understand the future because it's unknown and will continue to be unknown until it becomes the present. But our future is a memory to God, and he promises to take care of us in the midst of uncertainty (Matt. 6:25–34). If he takes care of the sparrows and the grass of the field, why wouldn't he take care of the people that he didn't spare his Son for (Rom. 8:32)? The problem that we have isn't with the gift, it's with the giver of the gift.

Jesus gives us such an amazing example of how to pray in the most distressing moments. He's about to be murdered while taking on all the sins of the world. He doesn't want to endure the cross, so he asks his Father to take it away. But here's the amazing part, he says at the end, "Nevertheless, not my will, but yours, be done" (Luke 22:42).

There's a song that has really helped me these last few months in becoming more surrendered and less controlling. It says, "I will make room for you to do whatever you want to, so do whatever you want to." When I am praying for my future now, this plays in the background while my palms are up and my fingers are stretched wide.

God, I pray that I will find a wife.

God, I pray this relationship will work out.

Enter your prayer here.

Here's the key: *But at the end of the day, let your will be done, not mine.*

That's why "palms up, fingers wide" has helped me. God can give and God can take away, and I'm praying that I will find peace in whatever he does. I'm praying I won't fight. I'm praying I'm humble enough when he gives and I'm trusting enough when he takes away.

At the end of the song it says, "Your way is better." When it comes to trust we're telling God that we *think* we know what's best for us, but he *knows* what's best. We may not see it or even understand it, but that doesn't mean he doesn't. "The heart of man plans his way, but the Lord establishes his steps" (Prov. 16:9).

Singleness is a gift that many people stiff-arm, but it's not the gift itself that we're not trusting, it's the gift giver. *No* is a hard word to hear. Our future is a memory to the God of universe. He sees things ahead that we are completely unaware of. There's a why behind every no, and just because he doesn't disclose it doesn't make him evil or the gift pointless.

In the story of Job, he's questioning God as to why God is taking away all that he loves. And God answers him in the way I have felt him tenderly answer me lately. "Where were you when I laid the foundation of the earth?" (Job 38:4).

No is never easy to hear. I remember the devastation I felt in the seventh grade. It felt a lot like the devastation of the last few months. In life's tough situations we can have peace, not because of our perspective, but because the giver of the gift of singleness is trustworthy. We may not be able to see why, but let's be honest, we never will.

So, in my singleness I choose to trust the one who laid the foundations of the earth rather than my limited and finite mind. There's the right answer, but it doesn't always make it easier.

Chapter 5

Gift Doesn't Mean Easy

Hard doesn't mean bad. Easy doesn't mean good.

I played soccer in high school, and during my junior year a new assistant coach joined the team and told us, "I can't promise we'll be the most skilled team in every game, but I can promise you we'll be the best conditioned." It's a cliché and coaches have such a love for clichés, but this coach said it *and* proved it.

We conditioned after every practice, and I'm not talking about sprinting there and back twice. I know this is going to sound dramatic, but it felt like all of those drills were created back in medieval times to torture people. If someone (most people) didn't throw up, it was a miracle. We hated it. There were even some guys who had anxiety attacks because they knew what awaited them at the end of practice. We were either all overly dramatic or the conditioning was brutal, but it was probably a little of both—though I'm leaning toward the conditioning being *really* brutal.

In the middle of our conditioning exercises, the head coach would yell from the sideline, "Come on, guys, one day this will all be worth it." Those words, despite the fact they were well-intentioned, went in one ear and out the other. Worth it? How in the world would this be worth it?

We continued the conditioning throughout the season, and we were winning a lot. But we were winning games based on the fact that we were just better than all of those other teams, not because we were in better condition. And as the season progressed, the conditioning seemed less and less beneficial and "worth it."

We made it to the state championship, and for the first time all year we played a team that was just flat-out better than us. They were faster, more skilled, smarter, etc. You name it, they were better. Somehow, by shear dumb luck, we forced the game into overtime. When the regulation whistle blew, our team ran off the field like we always did.

The coaches greeted us with the biggest smiles on their faces. They told us to look over at the other sideline. Every player on the opposing team was laying on the ground, breathing so heavily it looked as if they were about to have mini-heart attacks. It was the state championship. You ran faster. Played harder. You left everything you had on the field. Both teams did. The difference? Their team was dead, but our team had plenty of gas in the tank.

We dominated the overtime period, put a goal into the back of the net and won 3–2.

Our perspective changed about conditioning. When the next year kicked off, we told the coach, not only did we want to do conditioning again, but we wanted to condition more. We wanted it to be more difficult and brutal. Why? Was the conditioning easier? No. People still threw up and still had anxiety attacks, but we saw the benefit of it all last year. The countless hours of running were all worth it. We couldn't see it in the moment (in the middle of our lungs drowning in our own blood), but it was making us better, stronger soccer players.

My team and I realized if we didn't condition the way we did, we probably would not have won the state championship. There was a meaning to the madness and pain. The coach wasn't a sadist who enjoyed torturing high school soccer players. He wanted to win as badly as we did, and he was willing to take the "I wish you were never born" looks. What felt like a death sentence in the moment turned out to be the biggest blessing of our season. Conditioning wasn't easy. It was really hard.

It had to be.

There are more people with the gift of singleness than ever before, but why doesn't it feel like a gift sometimes (most of the time)? I thought gifts were supposed to be enjoyable? If not enjoyable, then somewhat bearable. I never opened a punishment or a chore under the tree on Christmas morning. If singleness is such a great gift, then why am I not leaping with joy at the thought of it? Why is it so hard? Am I doing something wrong?

Singleness is a gift to single people, and single people are a gift to the church. We focus mostly on the latter, which is incredibly important, but for some reason we ignore how singleness is as important a gift to the receiver of the gift. We say things like, "Singleness secures full devotion to the Lord," then we move on as if that answer is enough. It sounds good. It allows people to feel encouraged and hopeful. But there's more to that answer.

Is it true that singleness can secure full devotion to the Lord? You better believe it, but the way it can and will secure devotion (at least for me in my experience) isn't the easiest. In fact, it's really hard and very confusing in the moment. There are times it doesn't seem worth it, and I'm not singing the praises of the Lord. But just because it doesn't feel worth it and doesn't seem like a gift to me, it doesn't make it any less worth it or any less of a gift.

More than a Feeling

We live in a world that is no longer ruled by truth but by feelings. The number of times I have heard, "I just don't *feel* like that's true," is honestly a little concerning.

Singleness is a gift, but whoever said it was going to be easy? Conditioning my junior year never felt like a blessing. It was *never* easy. I never sang the praises of my coach as I was fighting to stay conscious and keep that day's lunch in my body. No, we said some pretty awful things behind his back and to his face. But just because it felt like a punishment in the moment, didn't make it any less beneficial or worth it, didn't make it any less of a gift.

What if one of the gifts of singleness is actually making it really hard? Making it not easy on purpose? To sit in the crud and be confused and frustrated and say, "God, if I'm being totally honest, I don't want to praise you right now. You don't seem to be in control. You don't seem to be good. You seem less like the shepherd who leads his sheep into greener pastures and more like the butcher who leads the cows to the slaughter, leads *me* to the slaughter."

What if in this gift of singleness God is moving us away from how we feel about him and closer to the idea that there is an objectified truth to who he is? What if he's showing us that he is good every second of every day? He is always in control and never leaves the throne? He is capable of doing anything, but will never give his children things that aren't what's best for them? What if he's showing us that all of those things that were true about him yesterday are still true about him today and will be true about him forever (Heb. 13:8)? Those things are true whether we're in a relationship, married, or single? When we get what we want and when we don't?

Will he still be worthy of our worship even when he doesn't give us what we want? Even when things feel incredibly uncertain?

God is more than a feeling, and because of that, the way we worship him should not be based on how we feel. But let me tell you, my worship and the way I feel are more correlated than I'd like to admit. When things are great and he's answering prayers, then my prayer life and my walk with him are incredible. I'm thankful and have no problem telling people about how good he is. But when things aren't going my way, when relationships don't work out, when my prayers seem to be hitting deaf ears, I'm not telling people about how good my God is. Why? Because I don't *feel* like he is. My prayer life struggles because I don't *feel* listened to or loved. I'm not thankful because, well, what the heck could I be thankful for? I don't *feel* like he's given me anything to be thankful for.

Not only is this *not* the way we were created to worship, but it reveals the selfishness in our hearts. It reveals the "what have you done for me lately" mentality. That's not love, it's selfish manipulation. I'll praise you when you earn it, and I'm the one who decides if you've earned it or not.

I wouldn't do this in any of my earthly relationships, but I do it in my relationship with the God of the universe. I do this with God who has poured his love into my heart (Rom. 5:5) and bought me for a price—his life (1 Cor. 6:20).

Our feelings are real, but they are not always (and I'm finding very rarely) reliable. Our feelings don't dictate truth. We may feel a certain way, but that definitely doesn't make it our reality.

Singleness is a gift for so many incredible reasons, but one of the things God has revealed to me in singleness is I can still praise him even when I don't *feel* like it. I can still believe he is good even when it doesn't feel like he is. I can still trust he is in control even when it feels like chaos is ruling. I can still believe he is working things out for my good even when it feels like there's no way he could be.

My love and devotion then move from an unreliable, fleeting feeling to an objectified, never-wavering reality. Our feelings change and morph, even in the span of a few minutes, but God has never and will never change. And what is the end result? A stronger faith whose foundation is cemented in who God is, not in our circumstances. And if that's the only gift of singleness (which it's not), then what a gift it is!

Humbling Toward Him Alone

All of that may seem great on paper, but when we're in the middle of conditioning, it is so hard to see and believe. When we're in seasons of pruning, God feels less like a Father and more like a bully. In the moment, we wonder how a God who is supposedly so loving could be so coldhearted.

There has to be a better way to communicate this point than kicking our feet out from beneath us and allowing us to fall face-first in the mud. Honestly, it can feel more like we went face-first into very unforgiving concrete. It's infuriating. It's confusing. "God, I thought you were good? I thought you were too good not to give me the best? There is no possible way this could be the best. I'm lonely. I'm heartbroken. Dude, I trusted you. You know I don't trust easily. And look where trusting you got me!"

I was mad—if you couldn't tell from my journal entry. But mostly I was hurt. Hurt that the God, no, the Father who's supposed to love and protect me instead allowed me to feel all of this. Allowed me to be twenty-five and still single when I have longed for marriage for quite some time. After I told God those very cruel (yet 100 percent honest) words, I was hit with a crazy reality. While I was down and hurting, I realized something incredibly profound. I was scrambling to get back to my feet. Embarrassed. Tears flooding my eyes. But as I was trying to catch my bearings, I looked up and Jesus was right there. Yes, I was hurting. Yes, I was dirty. Face-first, yes, in the mud, *but most importantly at his feet. The way I was created to be. A creation at the feet of its Creator.*

This was a time when my God complex got stripped and the reality of who I am was brought to the surface. We can think, in these seasons of pruning, that God is kicking our feet out from under us, knocking us down a few notches. But he's not kicking us down a few notches. He's reminding us of where we really are.

That's the key! That's what makes him so good and the act so loving. He's not demoting us. We've put ourselves in a place we were never meant to be, in a position where we were doomed to fail. The creation wasn't meant to be the Creator.

For the first time in my life I didn't feel strong enough. I couldn't do it. Did God weaken me? No, not in the slightest. But through humbling me, not only was God reminding me of who I was, he was reminding me of my strength and abilities. I'm not big on putting words into God's mouth, but one night I was really battling with this. I felt weak, alone, and incredibly confused. I just kept repeating the same thing over and over. "Why, God?

Why? I can't do it." And I just started writing. And clear as day it felt as if God said these words to me.

"You never have been able to do it. And you never will. Now, I've made it so impossibly hard for this reason. To show you who you are, to remind you of your abilities and your lack of strength. You aren't strong enough. You can't do enough to dig yourself out of this hole. And you know what? That's okay! I've known this about you all along. That's why I came and died. That's why I intervened. I had to. Because if I didn't, you would still be dead in your sins and trespasses (Eph. 2:1, 4–5), splashing around in the deep end, thinking you've achieved something, but really you were just drowning. You can't do it. Time won't heal it. But I can. I know this hurts. I know it's hard. I know you don't want to worship me as king because right now I seem so distant and so cruel. But will you *by faith* still worship me? Will you *by faith* still trust me? Will you *by faith* stop relying on your own strength and start relying on me as your rock and fortress and strength (Ps. 62:2)? Because it's then *and only then* that you are strong enough."

In our weakness, he is strong (2 Cor. 12:9–10). And here's the crazy part about all of this. All of us are sinful and prideful beyond our wildest imaginations, and if God didn't give us the hard times and gifts like singleness, we would *never* reach all of those conclusions on our own. It's when we realize this that we can see suffering and trials as huge blessings, even bigger blessings than marriage itself.

This is what singleness has taught me that I'm sure not many other things could. At least other things wouldn't teach it to me as effectively. *God's not just asking us to trust him. He's asking us to trust in him alone.*

And it took a loving Father to humbly remind me that trusting him also means not trusting in myself. Not trusting an earthly marriage to satisfy my longings. But to fully, 100 percent trust in him. The only one who sits on the throne. The only one who can fully heal. The only one who can fully satisfy.

Content in All Situations

One of the words I hear most in conjunction to singleness is the word *contentment*. I don't think there's anything wrong with that. But I think the problem lies in what our definition of contentment is. I think most of us define it incorrectly.

For some reason we tie contentment in our singleness with being able to answer the question, "If God wanted you to be single for the next ten years, would you be okay with that?" or "If God wanted you to [enter scenario here] for the next [enter any time period here], would you be okay?"

But why do we do this? I truly don't think this is the secret to finding contentment. We don't know what tomorrow is going to bring. Heck, we aren't even promised tomorrow (James 4:14). Contentment isn't found in a hypothetical future we aren't even promised. So why do we focus so much of our energy on this?

The apostle Paul gives us the definition of contentment in Philippians 4, and I know what just went through your mind. These verses are some of the most overused and misquoted verses in the Bible. And if you're like me, you've known people who have used these verses in hurtful and divisive ways. "God is going to answer your prayer because you can do all things through Christ who gives you strength." And then weeks, months, years pass, and God still hasn't answered your prayer. Theology matters. There are real people on the other side of Tweet-worthy, feel-good quotes that grossly misrepresent God.

I know people mean well when they quote Philippians 4:13, but that's not what these verses are saying. Paul isn't saying, "Jesus will give me everything I want." Paul says the exact opposite.

Look at verse 12. Paul says, "In any and every circumstance, I have learned the secret of facing plenty and hunger, abundance and need."

Don't just scan that. I truly believe there were times in Paul's life when he was starving. And I don't mean a "I skipped breakfast and I'm hungry for lunch" kind of starving. I'm talking about a "I haven't had food in days, and I don't know where my next meal is coming from" kind of hunger.

I'm going to guess Paul wasn't jumping with joy. I bet he didn't love it. I bet it wasn't easy. I bet he longed for a cheeseburger. But his longing to not be starving anymore didn't mean he wasn't content.

In the same way, longing for marriage doesn't mean we're discontent in our singleness. I think so many times we white-knuckle our way through trying to find contentment in our singleness because we're trying to put to death a God-given, good desire. And if we tie our contentment with our ability to put it to death, we will never in a million years be content.

Longing to be out of a hard or inconvenient situation isn't bad. It's not always sinful. It's what we do with the desire. It's with the desire we can ask one of the most important questions we will ever have to ask ourselves. The answer to this question is what reveals the state of our contentment in any and every situation.

We get to ask ourselves, "Is Jesus enough?"

I think contentment can be messy. And just like "gift doesn't mean easy," contentment doesn't mean easy either.

Contentment looks a lot like saying, "I would love some food right now, but even if I don't get any, it's okay because Jesus is enough" (Phil. 4:10–13).

"My God will save me from the fiery furnace, but even if he doesn't, I won't bow down to your idols, and I will continue to praise my God because he is enough" (Dan. 3:17–18).

"I know you're telling me to stop talking about Jesus or you'll have us killed, but we can't help but talk about what we've seen and heard. If we die or get beaten, so be it, because Jesus is enough" (Acts 4:19–20).

"If God never answers my prayer, I'll be all right because he is enough."

Do you think any of those things were easy? Do we see the three amigos in Daniel 3 running full speed into the fiery furnace? No. We see them being bound and then placed in the furnace. Why? Because it was really hard. I'm sure they wished they were anywhere but there, but no matter what happened, God was enough.

The secret to contentment isn't found in a future we aren't promised (James 4:14); it's found in being okay with where we are today. We don't need to continually ask ourselves if we're going to be okay with our singleness later on down the road; we need to be asking ourselves if we're okay with our singleness right now, in this moment. It's seeing, no matter our situation, that Jesus will always and forever be enough.

And if tomorrow does come, we believe whatever situation we're in that the Lord is going to give us the strength to face it.

James 4:14 doesn't just tell us we aren't promised tomorrow, but it says, even if we are blessed with tomorrow, it will be anything less than predictable. Life many times doesn't care about what we want. Life isn't dictated by our calendars; our calendars are dictated by life. Truly, we are all one phone call or text message from our knees.

Because, for most of us, we won't be single for the rest of our lives (which makes fretting over that question all the more ridiculous). But what happens when the unpredictable hits you square between the eyes? What happens when a routine doctor's visit turns your world upside down with the words, "I'm sorry, but your spouse has cancer." What happens when one day you're over the moon and painting the nursery pink and the next you're in the fetal position and reeling for answers, trying to wrap your mind around the fact that your baby girl isn't coming home?

Please don't think I'm a sadist. These are situations people in my life have lived through. And you know what both of those situations have in common? Neither of those families woke up thinking this awful, horrible thing was going to happen to them. Tragedy has that effect on everyone it encounters. These families definitely weren't asking themselves the day before, "Would I be okay if the love of my life got cancer or if we had a miscarriage?"

I'm trying to get us to see that the future is anything but predictable. The only day and situation we are promised is the day and situation we're in right now. Because, yes, we're one phone call away from our knees, but we're also one phone call away from unbelievable joy and happiness.

Asking the question, "Would I be okay if God wants me to be single for [enter time frame here]?" robs us of today's joy and strength (Matt. 6:34). We're asking the wrong question. The secret to contentment is found in the present. And when the unpredictable happens, when the uncomfortable happens, we can ask ourselves, "Is God enough?"

Is. He. Enough?

We aren't promised tomorrow. Life is unpredictable. But there is something we are promised. There is something that is predictable. I'll let Rachel from Desiring God take us home: "Contentment won't come from staring at the fact of our singleness but from lifting our eyes to a different horizon— beyond the what-ifs and if-onlys of the next few decades to the wonderful certainty that is thundering toward us. Even the best marriage is only ever a picture of what lies ahead for every Christian."

That's something we can long for and never be disappointed by. The fulfillment of this promise will be the fulfillment of who we were designed to be: worshiping God for who he is, the creation at the feet of their Creator, trusting in him alone, and finding our joy and contentment in our relationship with the risen Jesus. Singleness isn't easy, but what if part of its purpose is to help shape us into the people we were meant, no, created to be? One day we will see our Creator face-to-face and see that it was all worth it.

Chapter 6

Singleness in Action, Not Inaction

Playoff baseball. Win and move on. Lose and watch the rest of the playoffs from the comfort of your couch.

Coach called my number to pitch, and there wasn't anything to get me out of the zone. We got to the field, and I didn't say a word from the time we got there until I stepped foot on the mound in the bottom of the first. If you know me at all, that's really saying something.

I felt in control from the first pitch. First inning: three batters faced, three strikeouts. I walked to the dugout thinking I was Nolan Ryan.

The second inning was the same story as the first. Next two batters, two strikeouts. Nothing could distract me.

Absolutely nothing.

Well, nothing except a pretty blonde girl.

I got the next batter to no balls and two strikes. I was one pitch away from a perfect 2 innings. That's when it happened.

I heard my girlfriend's voice. She told me the night before she couldn't make it to the game. I looked into the stands and there she was, standing at the fence, obviously beaming with pride and drowning in her lies of "Sorry, I can't make it to your game."

I ended up walking the batter and then another five in a row. I was one pitch, one stinking pitch away from getting out of the inning, but I ended up being taken out, never recording another out and giving up 8 runs.

Safe to say we watched the rest of the playoffs from the comfort of our couches.

Those first five batters, I was on a mission. I couldn't hear the crowd, and it felt like the catcher and I were the only ones out there. Just simple pitch and catch.

But when I saw my girlfriend, my mission changed from trying to win the game to trying to impress her. Really, I went from "on mission" to "distracted" in the blink of an eye.

What's crazy is the apostle Paul in 1 Corinthians 7 says there is something that can distract us in life. Something that can cause us to be distracted from way more than a silly high school baseball game. Something that can cause us to lose our focus and become distracted from more than just throwing balls and strikes. It's something that can cause us to be distracted from our devotion to the Lord. You know what it is? Marriage.

Here's the incredible news though: no one is born married. Every person starts their life out as a single person, and singleness can promote undistracted, full devotion to the Lord and people. In other words, single people can play simple pitch and catch with the God of the universe all the time, while married people can be distracted by pretty blondes.

Undistracted, Fully Devoted

One of the most common ways people try to explain why I'm twenty-six and still single is, "Well, obviously you're just not ready for that blessing yet" or "God is just getting you ready to be married."

I smile and say things that I've already talked about in this book. But it seems like the Bible has a different explanation as to why I'm "still single."

Paul tells the church at Corinth he wishes they could be single like he is (1 Cor. 7:7), and he doesn't go on to explain it's because he's still in a season of growth and getting ready for the "big day." He actually tells them his singleness is a gift.

In fact, he has some things to say about marriage that somehow get left out of most sermons and podcasts and books. First, Paul tells them to avoid getting married if they can (1 Cor. 7:8). This can be a hard idea to grasp. One of the most common ways people avoid letting this sink in is they say they "burn with passion" so they don't feel like they have been given the gift of singleness.

If that's you, welcome to the majority. I also burn with passion. The question I have for you is this: Did you wake up single this morning? Take some time to answer the question, and after double clicking on that one and processing it with community, you'll likely come to the conclusion you did, in fact, wake up single. Guess what? You have been given the gift of singleness. I'm not even going to say today. I can't tell you how long you will be blessed with this gift. It could be months, years, even forever.

"Oh, you don't know me. I'll be married within five years."

As a fellow addict of telling God what my life is going to look like and as someone who told God I wouldn't write this book because I "wouldn't be single long enough," I just want to tell you that doesn't work out well. Truth is, we don't know anything about what the future will hold. What we do know is this: *If we woke up single, we have been given a gift. Embrace it and stop Jesus-juking away from it.*

Paul then says marriage causes worldly troubles he wants to *spare* them from (v. 28), and he adds that marriage is a distraction to our devotion to the Lord (v. 34).

I keep feeling like I have to apologize for saying these things. I think I have to remind everyone I'm not picking on marriage. Just because we hype up one gift, it doesn't mean we're trashing the other gift.

I know this is insecurity. I shouldn't have to apologize for what God has to say. Yes, marriage is a picture of the gospel and

God's relationship with us. Marriage is beautiful. Marriage is good (Prov. 18:22). But it can be (and oftentimes is) a distraction to our relationship with the Lord and other people. And this isn't something we should brush over lightly. Our purpose is to love God and love people (Matt. 22:37–40), and if marriage distracts us from doing those two things, it is a major deal.

Good things have their burdens too.

First Corinthians 7 sounds less like "I would save you from getting married too young when you're not ready or in a good place with the Lord" and more like "marriage is a distraction. Period. And I would spare you from that."

It almost sounds as if Paul is imploring the Corinthians to remain single. In my opinion, he seems to be begging them to stay single. You might disagree with me, but we can all agree on this: Paul is making the argument that the people who are best equipped to be dangerous for the kingdom of God are single people.

When I read 1 Corinthians 7, I hear the word *free* a lot. Free to serve our Lord in an undistracted, fully devoted way. Free to serve anyone at any time. Free to drop just about anything at any time. Free to live out the purpose we were created for in a more effective way.

This all comes together in verses 25–31. Paul tells the Corinthians to live as if they don't have wives, and reading that for the first time will cause your face to look like you just smelled rotten milk out of the carton.

Is Paul saying we shouldn't care about our spouses or, if you are married, we should seek to be single again? Not at all. Paul specifically says, "Are you bound to a wife? Do not seek to be free" (v. 27). So, what is Paul saying?

Look at verses 26 and 29: "In view of the present distress" and "the appointed time has grown very short." These statements act as bookends, and everything in between the bookends should be read with the bookends in mind.

Time is running out, but it isn't running out for you to find your spouse. Time is running out on this earth, and when that happens, no one will be married and all of us will be face-to-face with the one who has ransomed our souls.

The game is almost over. And if we're given a gift, we need to be using that gift to empower us to better live out of our purpose. Live in the light that time is running out.

When there is less time on the clock, we play harder and have a greater sense of urgency. Everything means more in the fourth quarter than it did in the first.

The other day we played Catchphrase as a staff. If you don't know the game, don't feel bad, neither did I. You are given a word, and you have to describe the word without saying it so the people on your team can guess what the word is. When your team gets it, you pass the device to the person on the other team, and they have to do the same thing with a different word. You come up with a specific amount of time, and if you are holding the device when the timer goes off, the other team gets a point.

In the beginning of the round, it's pretty chill. But by the end you're talking louder and faster. You're sweating more and talking a lot more with your hands. There's a greater sense of urgency. The time is running out, and you don't want to be holding the device when the timer goes off.

There's not much I fear more than having this life end and seeing my Creator and Savior face-to-face and regretting how I lived for his kingdom on Earth. I fear many of us are holding the device and have no idea the timer is about to go off.

Paul tells us how much time we have left: not a lot.

And our purpose is to live in light of this world ending. To make his name known in all the earth with a sense of urgency (Ps. 105:1). To make his kingdom come with a sense of urgency (Matt. 6:10). To go into all the world and preach the gospel to everyone as if our lives depended on it (Mark 16:15). To love God and love people as if our days could be over at any moment (Matt. 22:37–40).

When it's all over, we will all give an account of how we stewarded the gifts he gave us to progress his kingdom. What will we say about our singleness? Did we spend it obsessively trying to get out of it or did we spend it utilizing the benefits it brings for however long that may be?

There is something more important than your relationship status. Time is running out.

I'm Not Titling This Section Because You Wouldn't Read It If I Did

As I'm writing this chapter, I am a couple of months removed from my third breakup in the last year and a half. There has been loads of healing, and it seems like healing has come faster and easier than the previous two breakups combined.

I talked to my therapist about this, and it seems that healing has been more natural, not because I am getting used to dealing with a broken heart (that would be depressing), but because I have embraced my gift of singleness in ways I never have before.

After the first breakup, I started writing this book. This book was really just my grasping for straws, trying to figure things out. It became a journey to make sense of my singleness. I started finding answers, which brought some hope. I do have a purpose and there is a meaning to the madness. Then the second breakup happened. All of a sudden the answers didn't mean as much. Then the third breakup. I mean, Jiminy Christmas! Hope seemed light-years away. I felt more like a guy getting dominated by life.

That's when reality hit me between the eyes. This book brought answers, but I was the one who decided if I was going to live out these answers or not. Yes, singleness is a gift, but only if you're willing to use it. *Purpose only comes when you live it out, not when you merely know what it is.*

I realized for the last year and a half I was in survival mode. When I woke up in the morning, I would start my day with the mindset of "I just have to get through today" and then I would live out of that mindset for the rest of the day. I went to bed at night with that mindset, then I woke up with it and put the cycle on repeat. Days turned into weeks; weeks turned into months. It slowly just became who I was. This gave it the green light for selfishness to dominate my thoughts and life.

Survival mode placed me at the center of my life. It allowed me to enter into self-preservation mode because I was so worried of more hard being placed on my plate. And if I'm being honest, I couldn't handle more hard. Not another drop of it.

I wasn't reaching out to people because I was afraid of being rejected. I stopped caring about my friends and community who were hurting because caring means empathizing, and I can't even deal with my own hurt. So how could I deal with theirs too? It all seemed very overwhelming.

All of my attention was on me. I wasn't serving. I wasn't pursuing anyone. I wasn't praying for anyone. I had no purpose.

But with the help of some amazing people in my life, I decided to put my money where my mouth is and put my gift into practice.

I texted the dudes in my community and asked how I could bless them, how could I pray for them. I started babysitting their kids so they could take their wives on dates. I started running with a couple of married friends (I *hate* running) and made it my goal to ask them how they are intentionally loving their wives. I asked them how they were doing, because being a dad oftentimes means putting your feelings and desires on a back burner. I started meeting with some guys who were struggling and taking them out to eat in my free time. Yes, caring means empathy, but being single means I have the capacity and the emotional space to let in other people's problems.

Really, what I was doing was putting myself into more opportunities to love God and love people. And something crazy happened. For the first time in my life singleness felt less like a gift and more like a superpower. Now, I hope your eyes are okay. I know they had to have rolled *hard* after reading that. If I would've read that, I would've put this book down because I would've had it with this author. "I mean, bro, how cliché could you get?"

Please stay with me.

I had a superpower I wasn't using because *I was too afraid to use it*. Batman can't get hurt if he remains in his Bruce Wayne alter ego. At least that was my mindset. And it's true. If Bruce Wayne would've stayed a rich billionaire, his life would never really be in danger, but he also wouldn't have helped and blessed countless numbers of people.

I was frustrated with this stupid superpower. I didn't want to be able to drop everything because I wanted to be occupied with one person. And if I couldn't be occupied with one person, I wouldn't be occupied with anyone. How selfish is that? How opposite of "your kingdom come, your will be done" is that?

But not this time. After the third breakup, I looked in the mirror and said, "I'm Batman," and then I flexed real hard. Okay, I never said, "I'm Batman" (but of course I flexed).

I had a superpower, and it was time to use it.

The less I focused on myself, the more singleness seemed to be a gift. I have been able to personify something C. S. Lewis said: "True humility is not thinking less of yourself, it's thinking of yourself less." And because God works in upside-down ways, on the other side of selflessness and actually using my gift was healing, joy, and purpose. Which is very opposite of the self-help culture we live in today.

Single people, we have a superpower and we can choose to use it or not.

Can you imagine if Bruce Wayne would've spent all that time, money and energy on creating Batman, but he never went out to fight crime? Can you imagine Bruce putting on the Batman suit, ordering a pizza, watching a movie and then going to bed? He wouldn't be a superhero at all. He would just be a glorified comic con enthusiast.

What makes Bruce Wayne Batman are the things Batman is able to do that Bruce never could.

If we have been given the superpower of singleness but don't use it, we're a lot like a billionaire wearing a superhero costume and never leaving their house.

What can we do in our singleness that we wouldn't be able to do if we were married? If the answer to the question is nothing, then we're not using our gift. And if we're not using our gift, we're missing out on our purpose. *And if we're missing out on our purpose, then I'm guessing contentment is a pipe dream instead of a present reality.*

Bruce Wayne is safe. Batman is scary. But if Bruce Wayne never becomes Batman, he will never live out his purpose. It's when he uses his superpower that life and healing and meaning are found.

Don't Just Talk About It, Be About It

One of the hardest distances for anything or anyone to trek is the eighteen-inch journey from our head to our heart. It's easy to talk a big game about singleness being a gift but never really live it out. There are many days I don't want to use my superpower.

Don't continue making the same mistake I make on a regular basis: knowing the answers but not letting the answers penetrate your heart and life.

Imagine for a second the church using its superpower of singleness the way God designed it to use it. Student ministries, children's ministries, worship ministries, community centers, YMCAs, homeless communities, foster care organizations, homes of believers and nonbelievers flooded with single people willing and eager to radically use their gifts. Not wallowing in self-pity and wondering why God hasn't given them a spouse yet.

Single people. Let's put the self-help books down for a second. Let's stop obsessively praying for healing and contentment for just a moment. Let's put our pens and journals down, trying to process what we're feeling. Let's put the mirrors away, trying to focus on ourselves. And let's start looking out of the window that is the world and asking how we can love and be Jesus to our friends, churches, and communities. It's when we start living in this way that we find the contentment and healing we're desperately looking and asking and journaling for.

This right here has been the secret to my finding contentment in my singleness. For the longest time I was focusing inwardly on myself. "Where do I need to grow? How do I need to improve?" But the secret wasn't in self-reflection. It was in actually using my singleness.

I couldn't see it as a gift because I wasn't getting my hands dirty and using it as one.

We're asking the wrong question if we're asking, "Do I really have the gift of singleness?" We don't have a choice. We have it. The question we should be asking is, "How are we going to use it?" Or will we waste it along with the countless other resources we let go to waste for the kingdom of God?

Because if we're not going to use it, we will always struggle with our purpose.

We have the gift of being on the mound and being undistracted from worldly troubles. Will we use it or not? "Do or do not; there is no try"—Yoda.

Single people, we have a superpower, and it's time for us to stop talking about it and start using it.

Chapter 7

Lean into Your Loneliness

Have you ever had a time or situation in your life when the phrase "When it rains it pours" doesn't even begin to describe your reality? This was me a couple months ago.

After the third breakup, I was really wanting to be with people. There's something about being with people after a breakup that makes it not as bad.

Well, everyone was busy. Busy doing things with other people.

One night I showed up at a men's group and a lot of my married friends were talking about a trip to Florida they were about to take with their wives. A trip I would've loved to go on. I love the beach. I love vacationing. And I love the people who were going on the trip. Heck, I'm even from Florida. I wasn't invited because "You're single, and you would be the only single person there and that would be weird." It was really hard being the only guy in the friend group not invited.

I moved on from that conversation to another group of people who were talking about a trip to the Buffalo River they took that weekend. When I entered the circle, it was explained to me why I wasn't invited. This was fun. So, I left the men's group, counting that day as a loss.

A few weeks later I found out from a friend that a game night was happening the next day. Again, I had no idea this game night was happening. I wasn't invited.

Just four days later (yes, I know how many days later because this was pretty recent), I went running with some friends, and after the run, a buddy told the guy I was talking to that he and his wife would be late to his birthday get-together the next night. A get-together that, yes, you guessed it, I didn't know about. I received a "There is an informal ice cream eating tomorrow night; we would love for you to be there" invitation. But I felt anything but invited.

I don't share this so you should feel sad for me. I also don't share this to tell you I have horrible friends. In fact, I have incredible friends. The best a man can have. There were reasons I wasn't invited to some things which, after I had some difficult conversations, make sense now.

I share this to say, in the moment, none of it made sense. I felt rejected. I felt lonely. I felt as if I didn't belong.

And it's pretty common for single people to have similar stories to these. And it's even more common for single people to feel the way I felt.

The question is, what do we do with our loneliness? What do we do when we don't get the invite? How do we process it? Why do we feel it?

Loneliness is crippling. Nothing makes me want to run from God and people more than loneliness does. But fear not, if you are reading this and you're feeling lonely, welcome! So does almost every single person at one time or another. You are not alone. But there are answers. There is hope!

Lean into Loneliness

When we fear something, we don't ever think rationally about the thing we fear. Fear causes irrational thinking.

When I was a kid, I was terrified of the dark. And whenever I had a bad dream, there was only one place I could go where everything became okay and there was nothing to fear: my parents' bedroom. But I had to go through a whole other nightmare to get there.

An unrealistically long and even more unrealistically dark hallway.

On the opposite side of the house.

Where there was inevitably a man dressed as Scream, armed with a knife, ready to chase me as soon as I crossed the threshold of my room. (I accidentally saw a scene from that movie when I was very little.)

It was traumatic. Every night I had to set the record for the forty-yard dash for a three-year-old just to survive. I was forced to sprint.

Was Scream actually waiting for me every night to chase me, just to miss me right when I zoomed into my parents' room? No. Even if he were, he wouldn't stop chasing me just because I got into their room, and my parents weren't going to do anything about it when we both ran in awkwardly.

We become incredibly irrational when we're afraid, and the longer we don't face whatever's scaring us, the more irrational our fears become. As I grew up, I decided I wasn't going to run through the hallway. I would *walk* to my parents' room. My heart raced the entire time, but I did it. One time I even stood in the dark hallway, looked around, and allowed my eyes to adjust to see the hallway was the same hallway in the dark as it was in the light. I even turned around, and believe it or not, there was no Scream. I felt like Kevin McCallister in *Home Alone* when he's running outside his house and telling Harry and Marv, "Hey, I'm not afraid anymore!"

Now, as a twenty-six-year-old, when I go home and have a bad dream, I walk with no fear to my parents' room. *But it took facing the fear to acknowledge the irrationality it brought.*

Here's the crazy thing, fear isn't only reserved for the young. It follows us as we get older. And what follows with fear is the irrationality it brings.

Lonely. Think about that word. What emotions come to your mind when you see it? Does it paralyze you? Scare you? Does it bring up the past? The present? "That's the word that describes my life right now. I'm completely and helplessly lonely."

Everyone wants connection. Everyone wants companionship. Everyone wants a feeling of belonging to a community of people. I don't care how introverted you say you are, everyone wants to belong. It's hard-wired into us.

But for some reason we latch our desire for companionship and connection onto romantic relationships. And the longer we're single, we tell ourselves, the longer we'll be lonely.

"God, if I'm being honest, I don't think it's possible for me to be alone."

I can relate to this even now. But can I tell you something? That thought isn't true. You know what it is? The irrationality that fear brings into our minds.

One day recently I was wallowing in my "I'm alone and no cares" attitude when a family in the student ministry offered me their cabin for the weekend as a "Thank you for all you do."

First thought that came to my mind? *That would be fun to do—with a wife.* Yeah, I'm rolling my eyes too.

My mentor challenged me earlier in the week to "lean into my loneliness." So I did. I faced my fear of being alone. There was a lot of anxiety and fear going into the weekend. To say I wasn't looking forward to it is an understatement.

But during my getaway for one, I encountered something I never expected. I had an incredible time! I read Scripture and a book a friend recommended, journaled, fished, talked out loud to God, watched the sunrise, took a walk, and even took a nap in the middle of the day.

I realized I tend to surround myself with so much noise, so much busyness so I don't have to feel so alone. But by doing all of that, I have robbed myself of being alone *with God.*

I experienced him in a brand-new way at the cabin.

All of a sudden the irrationality of my fear of loneliness was brought to the surface. I stood in the dark hallway, allowed my eyes to adjust, and realized it really wasn't all that scary.

I'm not saying I never struggle with loneliness anymore. That just wouldn't be true. I'm also not saying we don't need people. We do. We're called to be in community (Heb. 10:24–25). We're going to get into how single people can find companionship in earthly relationships later in this chapter. And it's so true. Something God has used to change my life to help me in my journey to find contentment in my singleness.

But if that's all we talk about, we will miss what our hearts are actually longing for. Yes, we long for connection, but what happens *when* people are busy? What happens *when* people leave or even breakup with us or we breakup with them? Or, more important, what happens *when* people let us down?

Yes, we long for companionship, but if we think companionship is fulfilled in a person or people, we will be incredibly let down when any of those things happen that are mentioned above.

Too many times I feel lonely, and instead of leaning into it and facing my fear, I end up turning to Netflix so I can deflect and veg out on something to make me not feel as alone. But the same thing ends up happening every time I turn Netflix off: *the loneliness I felt before the veg session is not only still there but magnified.*

The weekend-for-one getaway was big for lots of reasons. It taught me there is a difference between being alone and being lonely. We have to address our loneliness and accept that distractions like Netflix and social media don't solve the issue. They only put it off.

Loneliness is actually an opportunity. Oh, yeah, I said it. Oh, yeah, I don't like it just as much as you don't. But it is an opportunity to remind us that we weren't created to be alone. We were created as God's image bearers and created to be in relationship with him (Gen. 1:27). Sin distorted that vertical relationship. Sin also distorted all of our horizontal relationships. So, because of sin, there are aspects of loneliness that will not go away until we're on the other side of eternity. But loneliness a lot of the time acts as a gauge to remind us that we need God and people. Loneliness can, at times, be the check engine light that tells us something isn't right. An opportunity that will go unrealized if we don't face our fear of it.

Afraid of being alone? Don't run from it. Lean into it. Face it. Go out to eat *by yourself.* Drive to an out-of-town coffee shop and read *by yourself.* Get an Airbnb in the woods for the weekend "with your bad self" (*by yourself*). And something will start to happen. As believers, we will start to realize we are always in the presence of God (Ps. 139:7–12). We are never alone. Pursued *always* by the God of the universe.

It's a scary thing to be alone, but it's time we stand in the hallway of our loneliness and let our eyes adjust instead of just running as fast as we can through it. It's when we face it that we can sincerely ask ourselves, "Is Jesus really enough?"

Depth and Breadth of Relationship

Let me be up-front about this section I am about to write. This is one of the last sections I wrote of the book. This has been one of the things I have struggled with the most in my journey to find contentment in my singleness.

I have struggled to find connection with my community here in Searcy. People have just gotten busier. I think, in the beginning, there were some hard feelings toward these people, but as I have gotten healthier, I've realized that their getting busier was all a part of life. My community added spouses, kids, jobs, responsibilities, etc. And it was and is completely unfair of me to expect my friends to abandon their families and responsibilities to be with me. Something I realize now but didn't realize then.

I held off writing about this because I didn't want to write something I wasn't experiencing. Not following Jesus until I was nineteen has allowed me to see the church from an outsider's perspective. And from that perspective, it led me to hate disingenuousness. Fakeness. People saying one thing from onstage (or in this case from behind a laptop) and living a completely different life behind the scenes.

I didn't want to write the answers just because I knew them. I could easily write about how I am experiencing so much community with people when I'm really struggling with finding what I know I *should be* experiencing. So, I held off and asked the Lord to reveal the truth. And, oh, buddy, was he faithful in answering that prayer.

You see, I only thought I was struggling to find community and connection. It felt as if God was holding out on me. But the problem wasn't with God. It was actually me and my sin that were the problem.

Yes, I have been struggling, but I have been struggling with being ungrateful, petty, and entitled. I have an idea of what my life is supposed to look like. Really, I have a requirement of what I believe God is supposed to do for me. I don't long for marriage necessarily, but I long to go home to someone every night. I long for someone to spend my free time with. And since there have been so many nights I have come home to an empty house, I felt as if I didn't have the community I deserved, therefore I didn't have community at all.

I blamed it all on God. Almost a "How dare you for forgetting me!"

But the only thing I was doing was robbing myself of the joys and blessings God was *daily* giving me. God has and continues to give me so much, but I wasn't thankful for all of those things because I was so upset by what I didn't have. Entitled meet ungrateful. Ungrateful meet entitled.

A few Tuesdays ago, we were having a staff Christmas party. Loneliness started creeping its way into my thoughts. I started to feel bad for myself because I didn't have a special someone there with me, like everyone else did. Immediately the Holy Spirit convicted me to just spend time thanking God for what I did have. How do you fight ungratefulness? With gratefulness!

It was crazy. There were so many blessings just that day I could be thankful for. Then I looked around the table at the people I get to do ministry with every single day. And all of these memories started flooding my mind. Funny moments. Crazy moments. Moments where I needed someone to sit and listen and be there for me and someone on staff was there.

In the span of five minutes I went from "woe is me" to "I'm so blessed to be sitting around the table with these people." I went from focusing on what I didn't have to being thankful for what I did.

Then I started thinking about my last week. The day before I had gone to a men's group with ten-plus guys I am doing life with. I share everything with them, and they share everything with me. The day before that I babysat two of my best friends' kids while they went to a community group. And before I babysat, I ate dinner with one of those families that call me "Uncle Ben." The day before that a buddy spent an entire Saturday with me watching college football. The day before that—

You get the idea.

My loneliness has been fed by my focusing so heavily on what I don't have and what I feel that God owes me, and I have been completely blind to what I've been doing. I have let it cripple me.

But I have community. I have people who love me. I have people who like me and care deeply for me. Just because I don't get invited over all the time doesn't mean any of those things are any less true. *Their busyness has nothing to do with my worth.*

And it may not be what you want to hear, but sometimes we don't have anyone to hang out with because we aren't initiating. A common characteristic of someone who feels as if God owes them something is someone who feels like people also owe them something. Take it from someone who recently realized both of those things are true about him.

We don't just use the gift of singleness in big ways; we can use it in small ways. Like being initiators. There have been many times I longed to be with my friends on a Saturday afternoon or a Friday night, and I waited for an invite that never came. It's as if I said I would only hangout with people if they were the ones who pursued me. Ha! Writing this out feels so petty.

I have two challenges for us.

First, when loneliness starts creeping in, pause and start replaying your day and thanking God for the people and the moments that came your way. Many times, we struggle because our perspective and our hearts are off, not because God has forgotten us.

Second, be the initiator in your friend group. Swallow the pride of having to be the one who is pursued and be the pursuer. I mean, what an incredible representation of the gospel!

And there may be times when you'll be able to put both of these into practice at the same time. Sometimes initiating is just the first step in getting the ball rolling for connection. It has happened to me quite a bit, but there have been times I have invited myself over and my friends couldn't hang. But they have always thrown out other times they could. In those moments I can practice thanking God and being alone with him as I wait to be with my community later in the week.

Marriage goes deep, but singleness goes deep *and* wide. And when we are ungrateful and too prideful to initiate, we will miss the depth and breadth of relationship singleness provides.

Belonging

This all sounds great, but what happens when we feel there's just a natural disconnect between us and our married friends? We have time to give and receive, and time is something they don't have a lot of.

But I have learned something recently that has been an absolute game changer. Disconnect due to our life stage doesn't mean we don't belong.

I was spending time with the Lord the other day and feeling this disconnect and sense of not belonging a little more than usual. And then a thought came to my mind. *You think there's a*

*disconnect between you as a single person and the married people
in your life? Imagine the disconnect between Jesus and his disciples.
Yeah, they all (except Peter) were single, but imagine the disconnect
between being God and not being God.*

Those opposing life stages never kept Jesus from being in
intentional community with these "not God" people. It didn't
keep Jesus from belonging. And here's the amazing thing: it
didn't keep the disciples from belonging with Jesus!

You see, there were many times Jesus would just disappear.
The disciples would wake up and find Jesus was gone. And it
doesn't look like he ever left a note saying where he was going. It
also appears the disciples didn't love it when Jesus did this, but it
didn't stop him from doing it. It was almost as if he didn't want
to be found. Why?

Jesus didn't want to be found because he was alone with his
Father. He was intimately in relationship with his Dad.

Jesus could belong to a bunch of "not Gods" because he first
belonged with his Father. All of his horizontal relationships were
flowing from his vertical relationship.

Belonging isn't a feeling. As believers, we belong in the family
of God. There aren't different types of people of God, such as
free or slave, Jew or Greek, single or married, but we are all one
body (Gal. 3:28; 1 Cor. 12:13). And we can take a page out of
Jesus' book in that we will never belong with these people if we
aren't first belonging to our Father. If we do it the other way
around, we will start putting heavenly expectations on people
who will never be able to fulfill them.

Here's the amazing thing about belonging to God. Yes, we are his, but he is also ours. We belong to him, and he belongs to us. I started this chapter by saying I didn't feel invited. We all long for an invitation to dinner. We all long for a seat at the table with our friends. But can I tell you something that is so amazing about the gospel? When we're not invited to have a seat at the table with our friends, we're invited to have a seat at the table with God as sons and daughters. Not only is the door always open, but God is always actively inviting and pursuing us to come and sit and eat with him.

We can even take this a step further. Not only are we invited to be a part of the table now, but at the end of all time, Revelation 19 talks about there being the marriage supper of the Lamb. And anyone who is anyone will be invited to this wedding. It's the wedding of all weddings! It's the wedding all weddings now are pointing to. The last wedding to ever take place. The wedding where Jesus will marry his bride, the church. And Revelation 19:9 says, "Blessed are those who are invited to the marriage supper of the Lamb." This is an invitation that won't get lost in-between the seats.

We. Are. Invited.

You see, here's the key to loneliness. We don't fear being lonely; we fear not belonging. We're fearing something we don't ever have to fear again. We're fearing something we've been saved from.

A spouse will never fill the lonely hole in our hearts. We think "I do" is the secret alakazam for our loneliness, but we know too many married people to know that isn't true.

That's why learning to cope with loneliness is so important. We have to practice being alone. We have to get away from the people we use as quick fixes and crutches to avoid loneliness. We have to get alone with God, the fulfillment of all our longings. Honestly, we have to start practicing belonging to God.

Seriously! Put your money where your mouth is. Stop underlining and talking about it and move into action. When you get home, leave the TV off. Get alone with God. Don't just do it once, do this for weeks and even months. Stop allowing yourself to numb out. Turn all the noise, all the distractions off.

You can even take it a step further. Go online and find a house in the middle of nowhere and spend a weekend completely disconnected, realigning your heart to the Father.

Get. Alone. With. God.

And once our vertical relationship is where it is designed to be, we can start truly experiencing the fruits of the depth and breadth of the relationships singleness provides.

It's time for us to stand in the hallway of our loneliness and say, "Hey, I'm not afraid anymore!"

Chapter 8

Breakups Suck, But It's Going to Be Ok

I've never been a crier. I can count on one hand the number of times I've cried in the last ten years. I don't wear this as a badge of honor. I'm just telling you this to show you how rare it is.

I had just broken up with my girlfriend of five months, and I immediately called my buddy Shawn. He dropped everything and told me to come over as fast as I could.

When I got to his house, everything was moving in slow motion. My heart literally felt as if it was breaking. I mean literally, like the muscle was being torn apart in my chest cavity. I was about to be the cliché of dying from a broken heart. I felt heavy, but nothing was playing in my head. Somehow, I felt so much yet felt nothing at all.

Shawn came out of his bedroom (I think I just walked in without knocking), ran (yes, actually ran) to me, and embraced me like a mother embraces her son coming home from a war.

Dude, I lost it. The next forty-five minutes I cried ten years' worth of tears. I couldn't stop. Tears were shooting out of my eyes. I finally calmed down, and I looked up at Shawn, who was also crying. All the times he had felt the sting of heartbreak were replaying in his head as he wished he could take it all away from me.

I thought I was done. How could I cry anymore? I mean there couldn't have been any more liquid in my body. It was all on Shawn's shirt. Then his three-year-old daughter came into the room and said, "Untle [she couldn't pronounce the *c* in *uncle*] Ben, I'm sorry. I love you," and then she rubbed my back. Ah, yes, there's the rest of my tears.

There's nothing that breaks like a broken heart.

This has been an ancient saying. It has stood the test of time because heartbreak transcends time. But it's only when you go through a breakup that it changes from a statement into your reality. In fact, in the middle of it all, the statement doesn't even come close to doing the feeling justice.

I wouldn't wish a breakup on my worst enemy. And unless you're in the middle of a breakup, you forget just how painful they can be.

There are not enough words, podcasts, sermons, or songs to make us stop feeling the crippling sorrow of it all. Our appetites go out the window. Even when we eat, food loses its flavor. The things we loved doing before are no longer appealing. We're sad and unbelievably angry at the same time. Everything we do, big and small, reminds us of our lost love and that they're no longer there. People try to tell us we just need to move on.

"There are plenty of fish in the sea."

"Forget them!" (As if we haven't been trying.)

"You were out of their league anyway."

"You just gotta get yourself back at there."

And God forbid anyone ever says, "All things work together for good." (We should have a free "punch in the face pass" every time someone flippantly throws that verse around!)

We know we need to move on, but we either can't or, worse, we don't want to. Moving on would mean trying to become okay with a future without them. And we're just not yet ready for that.

Really the worst part of it all is the feeling of a sudden void in our lives. The person we talked to all the time, spent most of our free time with, our best friend, maybe even the person we talked about forever with has not just taken a back seat in our lives, but they are completely removed, cold turkey.

It's as if we're grieving a death, but it can more painful because they aren't actually dead. We still see them. We just have to act like they're sorta dead.

And what's so unbelievably confusing about a breakup is the person doing the breaking up can be in just as much pain (even more sometimes) than the person being broken up with.

It's funny (not "ha, ha" funny, but peculiar) how God works. I have been on both sides of this very sadistic coin in the last year and half. I was broken up with first, and then about eight months later I was the one doing the breaking up. And what made me so confused is that I cried more breaking up than I did being broken up with.

"God, how can I be so sad? I knew this had to happen. Should this hurt so much since I'm the one who initiated all of this?"

There were times I felt as if I was actually going crazy. And no matter how many times my community told me I wasn't, it didn't make me feel anymore sane.

Breakups are almost inevitable for us all, no matter how hard we try to avoid them. As I write this chapter, it's still very real for me. Very raw. Very recent. Some days it's easy, and other days it's *impossibly* hard.

But there *is* a purpose beyond what most people (even people in the church) say. There *is* an answer to the question, "What do I do now?" And if we can take a biblical perspective on it, I know it will lead to our healing and save us from entering into even more heartache. Heartache that stems from mistakes most people make in the wake of a breakup.

Just Do the Next Faithful Thing

"What do I do now?"

In just a few short moments our lives are turned upside down. We're just trying to stop the world from spinning. We want answers, and we're desperate for them now.

"One day you'll be thankful for this breakup. It's going to make you that much more ready when the real thing comes along." Oh, my word. Someone needs to hold my hair back. I hear this statement All. The. Time. Do we really think the God of the universe allowed all of this to happen for the sole purpose of getting us more ready to meet our spouse? How one dimensional and boring would that be?

But do you know when that statement frustrates me the most? When I hear it constantly pulsating within my own thoughts.

I was talking with my buddy Andrew the other day. Both of us were fresh out of relationships, and we were grasping for straws to try to make sense of it all. We wanted answers, and we wanted them now. What's the purpose of the relationship not working out? Why didn't it? Is there something wrong with us? Are we incapable of love? Are we too picky? Will we always come so close to the finish line just to end it, go through heartbreak, get into another relationship, and just start the cycle all over again? The usual, light, "bring up at a party" questions. This also answers why everyone has always avoided us whenever they saw us talking.

Andrew told me he was listening to a podcast earlier about breakups. In the podcast they said now you get to focus on bettering yourself and to stop looking for "the one" and become the one your one is looking for. Stop looking for marriage and start preparing yourself for marriage.

It's one of those "Yes, preach it!" moments. If that had been said in a sermon, everyone would have their pens out, jotting it down in their journals so they could remember the words for their next Instagram post. But I had a moment with the Holy Spirit; this sounds good, but it's flawed. And it was as if the God of the universe was sitting right across from me and said this.

Don't prepare yourself for marriage. Follow Jesus.

"Wow, eight chapters in, you must be getting desperate for content, so you're going for a cliché!"

Stay in the ring with me.

The goal and purpose for our lives isn't getting married, therefore the goal and purpose for relationships not working out can't be to just prepare us for marriage.

For the longest time I have viewed breakups as God's withholding marriage. I really wanted it, and God was holding out. But the Lord wasn't withholding marriage from me just because a relationship didn't work out. He was actively giving me singleness.

Now, I know that statement could cause the average American Christian to shudder, because we have been taught that God takes a back seat when it comes to dating. As if God only cares about us not being unequally yoked, and then after that he shrugs his shoulders and says, "Everything else is up to them." *Why do we think God is sovereign in every area of life but dating?*

I am a firm believer that God opens people's eyes to each other, and, yes, I also believe God closes people's eyes to each other. People leave jobs because they feel as if God is "leading them in another direction." But when relationships don't work out, it can't be because God would lead anyone in that direction.

I don't believe God has one person for everyone. There is a long list of people we could marry today and be in God's will, but I also believe there's a long list of people we shouldn't marry either.

Now, a sidenote, please for the love of all that is holy, if you breakup with someone, please don't just use the excuse, "I feel God is leading me to breakup with you because he closed my eyes."

No.

Nope.

Maybe God did close your eyes, but the words, "I'm sorry, I don't see myself marrying you" or "I just don't like you like that anymore" go a long way. Unless you were absolutely crazy about them and you heard the audible voice of God from heaven say, "Break up with them." If that happened, then go ahead and use the God card in the breakup.

But at the end of the day, the relationship didn't work because God didn't want it to. Marriage wasn't in the cards.

Now that it's over, we don't need to be telling ourselves that it's just to prepare us more for when it actually does work out. Because if that's the worldview we take, then we're going to be looking frantically for our next victim. We don't need to be waiting for the next person; we need to be waiting on the Lord.

This has been my biggest hurdle after breakups. I want someone to fill the void left by the last girl, so I am immediately longing for someone else to fill it. That's why we need the perspective shift from "Okay, where she at?" to "Okay, here I am, Lord. Send me."

But here's the amazing thing about following Jesus. When we follow Jesus, we fall more in love with him, and we start looking more like him. A side effect then would be his making us more of the one that the other one is looking for. But it will do so much more. It will make us the friend our friends are looking for. It will make us the worker our boss and our coworkers are looking to work with.

When we follow Jesus wholeheartedly, we bring a little piece of heaven to every person we encounter, everywhere we go. A side effect of following Jesus can then, in turn, prepare us more for marriage.

It's great on paper, but how do we do this?

Just do the next faithful thing. Take it moment by moment. Ask yourself, "How can I be faithful right now, in this moment?" Especially in the days and weeks following a breakup, that's all you really can do. Stop trying to look forty-five steps ahead and see where God is leading you. Just find where your next step should be. Look at people as more than just a means to an end. Bring a little piece of heaven everywhere you go.

And since I believe God is sovereign, I believe as we are walking with him, he will lead us where he wants us to go next as we are palms up, fingers wide, and saying, "Here I am, Lord, send me." And, yes, that means I believe he will reveal when it's time to "get back out there."

Major Mistakes in "Getting Back Out There"

Most of us will eventually enter the dating world again. Wounds will heal. We will move on. But many times, we don't do this in a healthy way. There are some common mistakes I and others I have witnessed make.

1. I will be ready to date when I ...
[enter a date or goal here].

Here's the problem with that mindset. What happens when that date or goal comes? What happens when you finish reading through God's Word? What happens when you finish—let's find something completely random—writing a book about singleness? Let me tell you what I do. I finish the goal and then I end up running full speed to find someone. As if the reward for reading through God's Word or writing a book about singleness is a spouse.

Let me explain it another way. Basketball coaches, to encourage more ball movement, tell their team they can't shoot until they pass the ball ten times. This very rarely works. The first ten passes are crisp, people are moving the ball well, and then after the tenth pass, ball movement goes out the window and someone takes a stupid forced shot.

We focus on the Lord for this time period, but once the time period is up, our eyes go from looking up to looking around obsessively. That's not how God works.

As my buddy T-Roth told me recently, "We can't use God to get something from him. Transactional obedience is disobedience."

2. I'm ready to date when there's no prospect in sight.

I'm going to say something that is about to blow your mind. This statement alone will be worth the price of this book. Ready? *You can't date nobody.*

More eyes rolled than jaws dropped probably. But at the end of the day, in order for someone to say, "I'm ready to date," there has to be somebody for that person to date. Even in 2022, it takes two to tango.

So many people are trying to wrestle with the idea of if they're ready for a relationship when there is no relationship to process if they're ready for.

But the game changes when there is somebody. When the other 50 percent of the relationship comes into the equation, then the processing can begin. Yes, it's important to know if you're ready to date, *but it's just as important to process if the person you are wanting to date is ready too.*

Are you pursuing the Lord, living in community, living in a season of health? (I've also heard this as "Long obedience in the same direction.") Okay, check. You're 50 percent of the way there.

Is the person you're wanting to date pursuing the Lord? (This means more than attending church. Seriously! Don't just scan that sentence. I'm going to say it again: *This means more than attending church!*) Is the person you're wanting to date living in community? (The way to know this? Ask the people they're in community with about them. If there's no one to ask, that may be your answer.) Is the person you're wanting to date living in a season of health? (Again, ask their community about this too.)

Then and *only after* all these questions are asked, can you answer if you are ready to date.

Emotional readiness doesn't always equal a relationship coming in the near future.

I'm going to guess the apostle Paul was pursuing the Lord, living in community, and living a *long* season of health and obedience. But as we know in Scripture, when Paul wrote 1 Corinthians 7, he was still single. Whether he was married later in life or not, the purpose of Paul getting healthy, planting churches, and writing half the New Testament was to be a part of bringing God's kingdom here. And are you ready for this? Paul never, not one time, mentioned he was ready for a relationship.

Paul had love on the brain, but it was centered around *agape*, God's kingdom-first love, not *eros* (erotic) love.

3. Allowing the pain of past relationships to keep us from entertaining the idea of future ones.

There are times in our lives when entering into a relationship is a bad idea. We're not emotionally or spiritually healthy or we just got out of a relationship, so if anything did come up, we should look in the opposite direction.

I don't need to be leading a girl on when I'm not in the place to lead. And you can't impart what you don't possess. I need to pause and get healthy again.

But there are times when I am healthy and something could come up, and I would be ready, but I say, "I'm not going to be dating for a long time."

We're so afraid of getting into another relationship because all the other ones before this didn't work out. So, the next one will obviously suffer the same fate as the last.

I'll be honest, this is where I am right now. I have been the king of telling everyone, "I am never dating again." Every time I say it, people smirk, roll their eyes, and say, "Never say never." "Can't wait to share this story at your wedding." "You're so extreme, I literally hate you." But what these people don't understand is that I'm not saying this out of bitterness. I mean what I say.

I'm currently sitting on a plane and heading home for Thanksgiving. This is the first year I'm not wishing I had a beautiful girl sitting next to me to spend the holidays with me and my family. I never want to date again.

Literally ever again.

And it's not because I've dated bad girls. No, in fact, I've dated some great ones. Ones who checked a lot of boxes that I had. They loved Jesus. They loved people. They even checked the "not essential but would be a plus" boxes.

But you see, all of these relationships had a major thing in common. Not only did they all end, but they all led to some pretty horrible pain. Pain that lasted way longer than I anticipated or desired. Which, if you made it this far into the book, you're probably saying, "Yeah, we noticed."

I now look at future relationships as inevitably headed in the same direction.

So, the attitude of never wanting to date again isn't out of a spirit of wisdom and patience; it's protecting Ben from being rejected or hurt again.

What if God has someone for us during our sabbatical from romance? So many times, we live our lives as if we had a burning bush moment from God without the appearance of a burning bush.

You Don't Just Heal *from* the Past, You Heal *for* the Future

Now, I'm not skipping over the season of "I never want to date again" or pretending I didn't say it. I'll be honest, I'm not loving being here. I feel as if my friends try to talk me into wanting to be available to date again. No one wants to break free from this mentality more than I do.

I started writing this chapter with the pain from those recent relationships in my rearview mirror. It sucked. But I was okay they didn't work out. I don't wish I could go back and change anything. I learned a lot. They were great girls, but we just weren't great for each other. The healing process has done its magic.

At least I thought it did.

"You just don't want to date again cause you're still hurting," a buddy told me. But that's not the case. I've moved on from the past. Perfectly? Heck no. Some days still have a sting to them. But for the most part I have moved on. It's over. Never going to work again. It's tough but bearable. The problem isn't the pain of the breakups; it's the thought of having to go through all of that pain again.

I've healed from the past, but the healing process hasn't led me to heal for the future yet. And that's not a bad thing. It doesn't mean my faith is small. It doesn't mean I love God less than anybody else. It just means I need more time to heal. You can't put healing on a schedule. Everyone heals differently, and every situation is unique. But what this does mean is my buddy was right when he said I don't want to date again because I'm still hurting.

I think I've known it for a while, but I have been hurt, and I'm terrified of getting hurt again. And not only have I been hurt, but I have allowed the hurt and the fear that accompanies it to dictate how I live parts of my life.

There's a big difference between saying we're okay it *didn't* work out and saying we're okay if it *doesn't* work out.

So maybe it's time for me to say, "I don't want to date right now." Could that change in the future? Possibly. Probably. The likelihood is good it will.

We just can't be afraid to put ourselves out there again because of the possibility that it won't work. Every relationship won't work until it does. And honestly, praise the Lord for that.

Who wants to be married to somebody they should've broken up with? As my buddy Hunter said after I asked him why my last relationship didn't work, "Bud, it didn't work because it wasn't working."

Do you feel guarded? It's okay to answer yes, because I do. My friend has been trying to set me up with someone, and I feel walls as thick as miles forming around my heart.

The phrase I keep telling myself is *just be a blessing*. You don't have to always be pursuing to be in relationship with the opposite sex. You think someone's pretty great? You don't have to steer clear because you're afraid. Just go and be the person who wants to be a blessing to people.

Now, if they're not good for you, then steer clear for wisdom's sake. But if they love Jesus and are about making his kingdom come, then bless them. Then you can join them in their quest, and they can join you in yours in bringing his kingdom to earth. Which is the goal of all Christ-centered relationships. Whether you're friends, dating, or married.

When we are present and living in the present, we are the best at offering ourselves. It's when we start looking into the future and obsessing over what hypothetical future hurt can ensue with this present decision that we stop offering ourselves fully and we stop being a blessing.

There's nothing that breaks like a broken heart. True. But I believe I serve a God who holds my heart in his hands. God is totally good and is only capable of giving us good gifts. So that must mean I'm right where I need to be. In the present.

And letting that transfer to my heart is monumental. And that's why healing has been so great. The last few months I have watched (painfully slowly, I might add) that truth travel from my head to my heart. The Lord is working on my heart. I'm not there yet, but I'm trusting him in the meantime.

It's with that heart I can say, "Here I am, Lord. Send me."

Chapter 9

Conversations with Fellow (MVP) Singles

A few months ago, I bought a side table from an online discount furniture store. I was trying to fill the house I just bought and trying to save some money while doing it. You know, baller on a budget over here.

When the side table arrived at my doorstep, I was shocked with how small the box was and even more shocked with how many pieces it came in. I was about to build this piece of furniture myself.

Well, as I started separating the millions of screws and pieces of wood, I realized something vitally important wasn't in the box. There were no instructions. I didn't even know where to start.

I knew all of these components would somehow come together and look like the image on the box, but without proper guidance, the picture on the box seemed like an impossible reality.

We're eight chapters into this book, and singleness looks really good on paper. We get excited because we want so desperately to use our gift, but when we open the box, we realize we have no idea how to make what's in the box look like the image on the box.

Many people don't even know where to start.

Singleness isn't just something that looks good on paper. The reason I'm writing this book isn't just to give me and other single people hope that their life stage isn't pointless. I'm not just trying to give single people answers for when they go home for the holidays and Grandma asks why they're still single.

There is a life to be lived in singleness that is unbelievably exhilarating and life giving. Singleness isn't just a gift, but it *can be* a powerful weapon that makes the enemy shudder when it is pointed toward him. Sometimes we just need guidance (instructions) to get us moving in the right direction.

While writing this book, I've been able to meet single people who make me want to run through all the walls. They aren't waiting for God to bring them a spouse to start being dangerous for the kingdom. They're doing it now.

The purpose of this chapter is to tell the stories of these people. To tell other single people's stories of how they are using their singleness as gifts. And my prayer is their stories—stories of single people becoming foster parents, leading sex trafficking ministries, discipling hundreds of people, or being the hands and feet of Christ in a dangerous country—will spark an excitement in you. I pray you will read these stories of single people being faithful and think, "That doesn't seem too hard. I can do what they're doing."

My prayer is, as you read their stories, you will be encouraged and realize your life of singleness can look like the image on the box. In fact, it can look better.

Emily Utz and Sheetal Agrawal

Meet Emily, thirty-eight, and Sheetal, thirty-five. Emily is being faithful in her singleness by being a foster mom, and Sheetal is being faithful in her singleness by being involved in a sex trafficking ministry.

What are you doing in your singleness now that you couldn't if you were married?

Sheetal: It reminds me of a story a married woman told me. She said this one thing that really stuck. She was so sold out in her singleness for the Lord that she would walk down a dark alleyway without fear and pray, *Lord, I trust you with my life and body.* She trusted him completely with her life.

After she got married, fear would set in when her husband would go out of town. She realized when she was single, she had a crazy dependence on God, but when she got married, dependence shifted to her husband. And she saw the stark contrasts on how she prayed when she was single versus when she got married. Her interests and focus were divided.

And when I heard that, I remembered thinking I never wanted to get to that place. I always wanted to live dangerously and recklessly undivided for the kingdom.

There's too much going on in our world to spend our singleness just waiting for God to bring us a spouse, and when I stopped doing that, I started actually enjoying my singleness. Like on Friday nights, instead of coming home disappointed I spent another Friday night without a date, I am living out a passion the Lord laid on my heart to fight sex trafficking. I go into the sex trade in Dallas and talk to pimps and prostitutes in hopes we can convince the girls they're worth so much more and provide resources on how they can get out.

If you would've told me when I was twenty-two that in the next ten years, instead of being married, I would be working with the FBI, Homeland Security, and vice to fight sex trafficking, I would have thought you were crazy. But our God invites us into wild and fun adventures far beyond our imaginations if we're just willing to say yes.

There are a couple of specific stories that stick out to me with how God is doing this.

On one of our outreaches, we received info about a brothel nearby, and we passed that intel to our partners in law enforcement. They raided the brothel, saved a number of girls, and arrested the pimps.

That's the story everyone wants to celebrate, but the brothel raids are few and far between. And while we pray earnestly for them and celebrate them, my favorite story has nothing to do with a raid. It's a story that reminds me to just be faithful.

A few months ago, we saw a girl walking the track, and I wanted to go up and talk to her, but she told us no. We had to back off because that could have meant her pimp was watching her, and by not complying to her response, we could have put her in danger. I ended up going out the next night, and I wanted to go back to that spot to see her but wasn't able to.

We were stopped in a place about a mile away, and we randomly ran into that girl. She walked up to us and said, "I was really sad I couldn't talk to you last night because there was a glow about you and the people you were with." And in that moment, I remember hearing the Lord say to me, *You weren't able to talk to her last night, but she saw my light. Even if you're unable to talk to these girls, they're still able to see my light because my light is more powerful than your words. Your job is to show up, and I'll do the work.*

I just want to be faithful with whatever the Lord puts in front of me. Whether I walk into the darkness of corporate America or I walk into my unsaved family's living room and boldly talk about my faith or I walk the streets of Dallas to fight sex trafficking, I want to live in a way where I'm always trusting God to show up in big ways moment by moment.

Do we believe singleness is powerful and that God can use it to do mighty things? But do we also believe faithfulness is enough? If your story never gets shared, people never know what you're doing, and you sit across from that one guy or that one girl every week and teach them God's Word and then you die. Do you believe you being faithful was enough even if nobody knew it?

That's what we're signing up for whether we're married or single. Faithfulness has to be enough, no matter the result. For every raid, there's thousands of hours of no raids and no girls being rescued. We want to celebrate those high moments, but people don't see the thousands of hours it took for people to train and know how to gain good intel. The thousands of hours of seemingly no results. *But you don't get the raid without the faithful hours behind it.*

Emily: All of this just brought the book *Kisses from Katie* to my mind. It's about this girl who was twenty-five and single and adorable who moved to Africa and fostered children. So, all of a sudden that became the thing. You're either married and live in America and have a dog and a picket fence or you're single and you move to Africa.

We have to debunk that. Just because you're single doesn't mean you have to move to Africa or you have to become a youth pastor. I think single people do a really bad job of feeling like they have to fall into a bucket. You can be single and be a bomb vice president of a large company in America. I think the question is, "What are you doing that you could only do if you were single?"

It doesn't mean you have to be a missionary or move to another country. Those were just the stories that were told to single people for so long. Those are some options, but just because you're single doesn't mean you have to be that person or fit in that box.

For so long I believed because I was single that meant there was a lot of things I couldn't do. I thought in order to be a mom, the first thing I would have to do is be a wife, have biological children, and then I would enter into motherhood. What got me into foster care was asking the Lord the question, "Have I defined motherhood incorrectly?" And his response was, *Yes, I'm so glad you asked.*

I found myself grieving tenfold something the Lord wasn't asking me to grieve in my singleness. It was like the Lord was telling me, *Emily, I never said you couldn't be a mom. I just told you I wanted you to be single. Why are you saying you aren't going to be a mom? That's weird. I never said that.*

I was deducing things that weren't from the Lord. What I was doing was grieving a lot of things the Lord never asked me to grieve.

I was defining motherhood incorrectly for a really long time because I was in a box. And when the box of motherhood wasn't fitting into my world of singleness, it led to devastation. When I finally allowed the King of the universe to be a part of that conversation, it was life changing.

The Lord had wired me in a specific way to be a mom, and every time I tried to stall out on this and say, "It doesn't make any sense on paper. Being a single woman and fostering a child makes zero sense. There's no way it would ever work out," I had six women telling me I needed to keep moving forward. They had my back.

Now I've fostered two children, and this makes the most sense. I feel more equipped than even some of my married foster moms.

Singleness is about finding the thing you're passionate about and living it out. Comparison will try to steal your joy, but it's about fighting it and getting ahead of it. If I allowed comparison to win, I would've never been a foster mom. I brought it into the light and allowed God to reveal truth to me. Motherhood isn't just for married people.

The verse that has made a huge impact on my life has been John 16:20: "You will weep and lament, but the world will rejoice. You will be sorrowful, but your sorrow will turn into joy." I think we have to reconcile that our grief might turn to joy when we enter the gates of heaven. And if that's the day it happens, are we okay with it?

May we never live a life where we're waiting for that to happen. Waiting for us to be all God created us to be. Waiting for us to do what God is calling us to do.

Does that mean being single is easy? No way. But when you get so sad, so lonely, so hung up on this one thing that the Lord is keeping from you, so desperate for a prayer to be answered, you have to get outside of yourself. You have got to go and serve somebody else. If you just sit there and stew on it, you won't get anywhere.

Sheetal: I think it all comes back to are you trying to do big things for the kingdom or just be faithful? That's why it's important to find what you're passionate about and pursue that in your singleness. I think if you try and fabricate a passion, you're going to fail all day long because you're distracted. It's continually going to the Lord and asking, "Lord, what do you want me to do? Clearly you have me single. What is your plan?" And then just being openhanded, trusting that God isn't trying to rip you off.

A lot of times doing great things for the kingdom in our singleness isn't easy. It's actually inviting the hard into our lives. Think about fostering like Emily is doing. That's hard as a single person. A lot of times it's harder for her than if she were married. For her to go out to eat, she has to carry a twenty-pound car seat into the restaurant with a diaper bag by herself.

In your singleness if you are saying yes to things, you could be saying yes to some really hard things. Are we willing to enter into the hard things? And not only if you're willing, but *how* are you inviting the hard things into your life as a single person?

Ways to Encourage the Church

Emily: I think about how well versed the average single person is to talk to their married friends about marriage. The vows they make, how they're called to purity and oneness, ways they can be pursuing their spouse. And then I think about how well equipped the average married person is to talk through singleness as a gift to their single friends. "Well, I really don't know what else to tell you." We have to do a better job at equipping.

Sheetal: If I were to have a microphone to try and edify the church on singleness for married folks, I would say to invite single people into your family. It doesn't have to be a nice dinner. It doesn't have to be a double date. Invite them regularly into the chaos.

What we desire is community. "It is not good that the man should be alone" (Gen. 2:18). I had a girl tell me the other day that she feels like she should've been married by now because it's not good for man to be alone.

That's not what that verse means. We were created to live in relationship, first with our Father and then others. We weren't created to live in isolation. We long for that family unit, and that's where married people can come in and invite those single people into their lives and their family. The church is supposed to be our family. And for us singles, we have to be better at initiating and asking our married friends to be a part of their lives.

Melissa Miller

Meet Melissa Miller, fifty-two. She would be upset with me for saying this, but I have never met such an encouraging person in my life. Everyone in this chapter has been a huge blessing to me, but every time I talk to Melissa, I'm more kingdom minded afterward than I was before our conversation. She is someone I look up to because, if there is anyone I could point out that is radically using their gift of singleness, it's her.

She has discipled hundreds (close to a thousand) people. Something she would not have been able to do if she wasn't single. Talk about the gates of hell shaking and the devil shaking in his britches every time she gets out of bed in the morning. I hope you are as encouraged by her as I am.

Melissa's Process to Contentment

I am very content in my singleness. I don't look at my life through the lens of my singleness. I view my life as the one that God has stewarded to me. And I'm very content in it.

Why am I content? Well, I haven't always been that way.

When I was thirty-six years old, I was the women's director of student ministries at Watermark, and I had been discipling women for close to sixteen years. I was single and very much didn't want to be single. I was struggling in my singleness and was really struggling with how God could continue to allow me to be single. I was doing all of the external things people tell you you're supposed to do to get married without success. I was still very much single. All the while, internally, I was fighting sadness as the clock was ticking on the years of my being able to have children.

I went to the doctor for my yearly checkup, and it was found that I had cervical cancer. Record scratched. Wait! What? I was told I was going to have to have a hysterectomy. It was too dangerous not to. That day, leaving her office, I knew why they called it a hysterectomy, because I was hysterical! I could not believe this was the story God was writing.

I remember so distinctly driving down the highway on my way home so angry at the Lord. "Are you kidding me? I love kids. I counsel women who have multiple kids who are not great mothers, and you're letting them have six kids? And me, the one who has been serving in student ministries, loving kids for the last six years, you're not going to let me have any?" While my response was full of pride and entitlement, it was the raw response of my heart in that painful moment of reality.

But on that drive home, a verse from Job came to mind. "Though he slay me, I will hope in him" (Job 13:15). And I felt God ask me a question, *Melissa, are you going to trust me when you can't have your own kids?* And I told the Lord, "I don't know. I'll get back to you." I was pretty ticked.

A few days later I told the Lord that I was angry, but I also told him I was going to do the work with him. He had so radically changed my life, and he deserved my effort.

For the next two weeks I wrestled with the Lord through prayer and searched Scripture. During that time I was able to look back on my life, and I saw how he chose me. I could not have chosen God on my own. I saw the way he led me to the job I was in at the time. I saw all the Scripture he had laid on my heart to get me through all of those years. And most importantly the fact that he gave me himself, that was the greatest gift I never deserved. And if that's the only gift I get in this life, it's enough. He is enough. If he's enough when I can't have kids, he's enough in all other areas of my life. He's enough in my singleness.

I came to the conclusion that he's either all good or not good at all. And after looking at all the times he'd stepped into my life, the way he initiated with me, not the other way around, I realized he's all good. The wrestling led me to a season where he really became my greatest reward. It really is better to be with him one day than a thousand anywhere else. Than a thousand days as a married person. Than a thousand days as a mom. Really and truly, being with Jesus for one day would be better than any of those things.

Now, that doesn't mean life has been easy or I don't struggle with things or I don't struggle with disappointment. I grieve not having a family. I did student ministry for sixteen years, of course I love kids. Within contentment I've had grief also. *Because contentment doesn't mean we don't experience grief over things our hearts desire on this earth.*

But I'm not longing for when or if that day will come. Because I truly believe where I'm at today is a gift he has given me for today, and I'm not promised tomorrow. If he's got marriage for me when I'm sixty then I'll embrace that. Right now, I'm just following him with what he's putting in front of me in that moment.

And please don't make me sound super spiritual, because I'm not. But since that moment, I have not struggled with contentment in my singleness.

What about the People Who Don't Want to Be Content in Their Singleness?

The hard truth of that is, it reveals our lack of belief. Not our macro-belief, but our micro-belief. "Yeah, I don't really believe you're good enough to be my everything." That's just saying we need something on this earth to make us feel better, to make us feel worthy, to make us believe we are who God says we are.

When you are saying, "I don't want to get to that place. I don't want to be single at fifty-two," you are revealing what your heart truly believes. You are showing you believe life is found here in marriage or in getting to have kids.

God in his kindness (not everyone believes it's kindness) is going to allow us to experience loss and suffering. It's not because he's mean, it's because he's so dedicated to getting us into that intimate relationship with him where he knows we will find our greatest satisfaction and fulfillment. Where he is our greatest desire, and we believe fully that he is who he says he is, and we are who he says we are. He's willing to do whatever it takes for us to get to that place, because he knows he is the greatest gift and the greatest reward. And he knows how our affections are so easily tempted to believe the things of this earth are our greatest reward.

I tell people, "I know you have this desire to get married and have kids, but the question you have to ask yourself is, 'Is it a desire above where God intended it to be?'" And that's a hard question to answer. Our minds want to say God is our greatest reward, but our actions a lot of the time don't back it up.

It's hard to address why a person is struggling with contentment without their sitting in front of me because there's so much to assess in that longing. Longings are not bad. It's how we respond to those longings that reveal division in our relationship with the Lord.

"I don't know how a loving Father could withhold marriage from me." Let's talk about that. That is way more important than this issue of your singleness. If you don't see a heavenly Father who reached down, chose you, put eternity in your heart (which you wouldn't have had on your own), chose to suffer in the most excruciating of ways so you could be in relationship with him, and you struggle to see that he is good and trustworthy, let's talk about why. What in your life has led to this point? So, it's a little more complicated than just a quick answer.

It all goes back to a crisis of belief. I understand your struggle in a very literal way, but you are showing where your heart really is in regard to being a disciple of Jesus. And, man, I get it. I get the fear of not being chosen. That struggle is real, but when you put your faith in Jesus, was it so that it looks good on a résumé or so you could get good things from him? Or is it because he's the pearl you have to sell everything you own to get (Matt. 13:45–46)? When you really know and trust the one who died for you, you understand how fully chosen you are.

Blame whoever you want, but we haven't done a good job of helping people recognize the beauty of the kingdom of God. If we knew the beauty and depth of his love for us, we'd be willing to give up anything to follow him.

We are in a battle because there's an enemy going, "Hey, you don't need to trust him. He lied to you. There's a much better life over here. Just go get that apple, it's going to make your world go round." That's the trick he's been using since the garden. And he still uses it. "You don't want to be single. There's a so much better life out there than that. Go chase it." In essence the enemy is telling us to turn away from the fountain of living water. The enemy is telling us to create our own cisterns (Jer. 2:13).

God calls that evil. This is why discipleship is so important. We need people to be telling us we're looking through a lens that the enemy wants us to look through. Because that's what's happening. We're buying the lie that life is found as soon as you get married. You and I both know way too many married people who tell us, "Yeah, about that. That's a bunch of hooey."

A lot of times we are where we are because we're not believing God is who he says he is. We're not believing we are who he says we are. And we're not believing he's going to do for us what he says he's going to do for us. We have turned away from the fountain of living water, and we're trying to get life from broken cisterns that can't hold water.

How Have You Seen God Use Your Singleness?

The thing that comes to mind is the amount of investment that I've gotten to do in discipling women. Pretty early on in my walk, I had the epiphany of, "Wow, God was going to let me teach women about him." It's an amazing privilege I have not gotten over.

I've also been able to see God redefine family for me. Before, I had a very traditional view of a family. Get married, have two and a half kids, live in a great house, and go to church. That was my idea of family. But in my singleness and the way I'm investing in women, God has brought women into my life who have not had good families or have experienced abuse or have lost Mom and/ or Dad. God has given me the privilege of becoming a spiritual mom to them.

I'm discipling a girl right now whose family of origin was really tough. She experienced abuse as a child. Her biggest struggle is feeling like nobody wants to choose her.

Through our time together, I have watched her grow in believing God is enough. And watching her image of God change because of that continual investment. It's been almost four years. It's not like we met and she changed overnight. The level of hurt she experienced as a child was so significant that it's taking time for God to restore the years the locusts have taken from her (Joel 2:25). God opened my heart toward her and gave me a love for her and really gave me a daughter I never had.

She has now become a part of my family. She is invited into every area of our lives: holidays, parties, etc. When we have a party, she helps host. When she wants to have a party with her friends, she has the party at our house. I am watching God use my family to restore her image of him. And that's one of the most miraculous things I have ever seen.

What a gift to be able to pour into somebody who has never felt chosen because of their family of origin and be able to look at them and say, "I choose you." And to be clear, I experience joy in this because I am not the answer they need. I get to point them to the answer. I get to say I choose you because the God of the universe chose me, and then model for them that love he extended to me and has in lavish supply for them (Eph. 1:8).

If I could say anything to single people, it would be, "Yes, use your gift of singleness. Sit across from people and point them to the answer. But life isn't found there. Life is found in the one who will never stop choosing you. Don't just point other people to the answer, remind yourself of the answer every single day. It's the only place you will find life."

"Bob"

Last but certainly not least, meet "Bob," sixty-five. Due to the sensitive nature of his work, we have to keep Bob's identity and the countries he's been in hidden.

How Did God Lead You to Move to This Country?

For me, God oftentimes speaks to me through TV and movies. I was in Bolivia, minding my own business. I had found my own apartment, and I thought I would marry a Bolivian and live happily ever after in Bolivia.

I was watching a news channel that was exposing some things about different places in the world. One particular night, it talked about drug addiction from the country I'm in now. And I was floored. A Muslim country has issues with drug addiction? It really hit my heart because of how closely I worked with addicts in the past. It showed mothers lighting opium to quiet their kids. It showed the opium pickers getting hooked because it gets in their system from picking it. Ten percent of the country is addicted to this drug.

I bawled like a baby after the program. I felt led to pray for this country. So almost every day I would pray, *God Almighty, please help these addicts. God, raise up some workers to go there.*

I'm already in Bolivia. It's not in my wildest imagination to go there myself.

So, I'm praying daily for these people and this country. One day I met some college students in a cafe from this country. That's when the dominos started to fall. These college students knew other college students from that country. Now, in the back of my mind, I'm going, "Whoa, what is going on here? I'm praying for this country, and now I'm meeting people from there."

About a year later I felt God ask me, *Are you willing to be an answer to your prayers for this country?* And my immediate reaction was no. No. No. No. NO. That is not happening. I've seen pictures of this place. I'm not going back to the twelfth century. This started a yearlong battle and wrestling match with God. And gently but surely he started upping the pressure. He kept saying he wanted me to go, and I kept saying it wouldn't happen. I was emphatic that I wasn't going there. At that point I'm fifty-eight. It took me forever to learn Spanish. I'm not learning another language. I don't have a heart for Muslims. I kept thinking God had the wrong guy.

I came back to the States because one of my jobs in Bolivia was selling jewelry for prostitutes (you have to love God's sense of humor). I was at YWAM and gave my update and how they can be supporting and praying for us. I was supposed to go to Dallas to meet a lady who helps us sell our jewelry and to talk to her about coming to Bolivia to see what she's helping to support. But before I could leave, a guy from YWAM stood up and said, "There's something else we need to be praying for you about."

And he kept pressing, even though I was telling him there wasn't anything else. He said he just knew it in his heart.

Now, I'm mad. I didn't even want to say the word. I knew the Holy Spirit was prompting me. And so, I finally told them "that country." And they all gasped. "God's been speaking to us for three months that he wants to raise somebody up from this base to go to that country." And I submitted, you'd think, right? Nope. I said, "You got the wrong guy. We can pray right now. I'll even pray with you. But I'm not the guy." And I was steaming inside. All the way to Dallas I am fuming with God.

I get into Dallas and I'm now talking to this lady, trying to promote her coming to Bolivia. And she says, "It would have to be at the end of April after I get back from"—yep, you guessed it—"that country."

We were in a cafe, and I punched the table. I was angry. And I just kept punching the table and yelling the name of the country. "What is it with that country?" And she was so confused and asked what was going on. And I told her, "I don't know, but everywhere I go that country is there."

Finally, I gave in, and I told her I wanted to go with her to that country. I just thought I needed to get it out of God's system. Surely if I went, he would realize I wasn't the guy. And what's crazy is, right before we were supposed to go, she backed out because terrorists blew up the community center where Christians met and some missionaries were killed. And her contacts in the country tried to talk me out of going. But at this point I'm going. Now God has all my attention, and I'm all in.

I ended up going. On my second day there, two people from my organization were killed and I felt a prevailing peace. I then knew this is where I needed to be. Doesn't mean I was happy about it, but I knew that I knew this was my next stop. Everyone else was freaking out, but I had peace.

I'm thankful we have the liberty of wrestling with God. I tell Muslims all the time, "Your religion is based on submission without question. My religion is based on Jacob, who becomes Israel, the man who wrestles with God." Yes, we finally obey, but God gives us the liberty to wrestle with him. And I am on the WWE circuit with God. And people think I'm trying to be humble, but I'm not. I'm the biggest whiney, crybaby missionary, but I eventually do it.

What Are Some Ways You've Seen God Moving Through You Over There?

(Due to the sensitive nature of this story and the danger it could cause, we have to keep identities hidden. This is one of Bob's many stories.)

There was a leadership class I taught in this country, and after every class we would have coaching sessions. And most of the time they would just want to know how they could learn English better or how they could get out of the country or how they could get a better job. But one young man, whose name was Besir, approached me and asked, "How can I get closer to God?"

I started meeting with this student one-on-one, encouraged him to pray in his own language, gave him a Bible, and gave him many books, including one titled *A Beautiful Way*.

A couple of weeks later, he sent me a text message asking if I could call him because he had been crying for three days. So, I called him up, and he said, "The book you gave me is just a profound book. I love this man's story and how he met God at fourteen years old skipping stones. How he had been trying so hard to please God, but how he had this revelation that God loves him just as he was."

And he read about how we are to love our God with all of our heart, soul, strength, and mind and how we are to love our neighbor as ourselves. And Besir said, "You know, when I read this, I'm so encouraged, but then, when I put it away, I just realize if I followed Jesus like you do, I'm going to get killed. Or at the least my family will be totally shamed and disown me. No one from my tribe will ever marry me. I'll be an infidel. I have all these dreams of being rich, but I would lose my job and lose my future. I would lose all these things I want. I want a God who makes my life work. Who does what I want. Who helps me and makes my life blossom and fulfills all my dreams. I use God. I don't love God with all my heart. And when it comes to people, I use them too. I don't love people. I'm just so broken by how completely selfish I am. I realize that my whole life revolves around me. Bob, I thought you said this was good news?"

I said, "Besir, you're so close. My book says, 'Blessed are the poor in spirit, for theirs is the kingdom of God' (Matt. 5:3). You are so close my friend. The gospel is a two-edged sword. First, it shows you your true heart. You're a sinner. You're selfish. You're not the good man you think you are. You're deeply flawed. But the second part, the great news, is there's a Savior to cover that. And to set you free from that. And to teach you how to love God. And to help you love your neighbor as yourself."

That was kind of the end of the conversation, and he said he needed some time to think about these things.

A couple of days later, he shows up in my city and comes to my apartment and says, "Hey, I'm in. I've counted the cost, and I want to follow God the way you do." Besir now follows Jesus because he sees that Jesus is worth it.

Single people, we have to get moving. My life hasn't been easy, but I have seen God do some unbelievable things. And having my own God stories is more precious to me than anything I could've been given in this life. I remember early on hearing all of these God stories, and I prayed, *God I want my own God stories.* He must've been laughing in heaven when I asked, saying, *Oh, son, you're going to get them, but I don't think you know what you just prayed for.* But truly, those are priceless to me. Because I don't just have faith in the Bible (which I do, it's the unerring Word of God), but I have, not just Bible stories, but my own stories of how he is real and how he hears me.

People try to feel sorry for me in the country I'm in right now, but I feel sorry for pew sitters. Where the only God they know is the God they see on Sundays. Where they're just trying to get God to make their life more comfortable. I have seen God do some radical things, and there's nothing in this life that is much better than that.

I would rather be a Peter who steps out of the boat and sinks because I got scared, but I would have the experience of walking on the water. I don't want to be like the other eleven who just watched. I want to be Peter, even if that means I screw up. The other eleven probably laughed at him when he got back in the boat. And I bet you Jesus said something like, "Yeah, but at least he stepped out." If Jesus says go, I want to step out. I may go shaking and trembling like I did coming over to the country I'm in now, but I want to go nonetheless.

Chapter 10

Q&A with
Jonathan "JP" Pokluda

I think it's beautiful the way God designed discipleship. Not only do we need community, but we need people who have "been there, done that" and are wiser than we are to help direct us in life.

The power of this book has centered around vulnerability: "I'm there with you."

But I don't want this book to be just single people talking to single people about singleness. I think if that's all it was, it would lack the depth a book like this requires. Yes, there is power in authenticity and vulnerability, but there is also a lot of power in wisdom. There's a lot of power in someone who has "been there, done that" sharing their wisdom in what they have learned in their singleness and what they are currently learning in marriage.

I have a lot of questions that are better answered by people who have experienced those things in their past. They learned how to answer these questions because they have already navigated that minefield and have used their experience to help other people, who are still in the minefield, find their way through it.

This chapter is a product of many talks with my friend Jonathan "JP" Pokluda. He is the lead pastor at Harris Creek Baptist Church in Waco, Texas. Before he was the lead pastor there, he worked with young adults at Watermark Community Church in Dallas through a ministry known as The Porch. He is the best-selling author of *Welcome to Adulting Outdated,* and *Your Story Has a Villain.* And the man is passionate about singleness and single people.

JP has an abundance of wisdom, but I asked him to be a part of this because of the number of years he spent ministering and counseling single people. He has seen the lies single people believe and has counseled thousands of single people through them. He's also seen the common mistakes single people make and has seen many single people use their gifts well. So, he has the wisdom and experience of working with single people but also the benefit of being married for seventeen years.

He helped answer questions about dating, "getting back out there," loneliness, pursuing purity in singleness, and so much more. JP has been there, done that, and I pray his wisdom can help us avoid some mines as we try to walk faithfully through the minefield.

Fear of Getting Hurt Again

Me: What would you say to people who are scared to date again?

JP: I would say, "Great, don't date again. You don't have to." Jesus was single. Paul was single. I think the problem is that you really want to be married, but you're just afraid because you don't want to be hurt again.

Well, if that's the case then you're just not ready for marriage, because you get hurt a lot in marriage. You haven't experienced the level of pain that's coming for you in marriage. The pain that exists in marriage is exponentially greater than the pain you just experienced in that breakup. And that can be pain in the relationship, missed expectations, challenges with in-laws, a miscarriage, parenting disagreements, financial hardship, etc. All of those things can create significant pain in the heart.

So, if you're saying, "I don't want to go through that again," that's just the Lord's kindness saying you're just not ready for marriage.

Me: Just to play devil's advocate, yes, there is a fear of getting hurt again. That definitely exists. But there's also a hesitancy for single people to get back out there again, because in the past relationship you poured out so much and were vulnerable with that person just for that person to leave.

And what I've heard from my own thoughts and from many single people is, "Well, at least in marriage they can't leave. I don't have to worry about pouring so much and having to start over with someone else."

What would you say to people who have the mindset of "Well, at least they won't leave."

JP: Yeah, one thought is, in a dating relationship, to not let your feelings progress beyond reality. We date like we're married and we go all in. The emotions are flying, the feelings are there. We are holding hands and spending lots of time together. I just wouldn't do that until you're confident this is headed to the altar, which is so radical. All of that sets you up for heartbreak. And I think dating today looks like having a death grip at every turn. "Where is this going?" "What's next?" "Do you agree?" "Where are you?" "I'm thinking about ring shopping. Is that where you're headed too?" And just every day making sure you're in the same place. And dating for as short of a time as possible.

And then for the people who go into marriage like, "Okay, I gotcha now, you don't have an out." That's why the divorce rate is 50 percent. They stop dating. They stop pursuing. They stop trying.

Really, you should save all of your real pursuing, all your buying flowers and writing poems and leaving voice mails for marriage. That's where that stuff belongs. People put their best foot forward in dating because that's the interview. And I think that's what sets them up for failure.

Me: You say not to chase feelings. What about the people who are feelers? How would you encourage them to navigate dating?

JP: Here's the deal, Ben. Here's my belief. Everything you believe about dating is completely wrong. It's made up. It's a 120-year-old euphemism for prostitution. Dating as you know it is not a good thing.

Do I know people who have done it right? Absolutely. But they are considered weirdos. They aren't chasing a feeling. Everything you've been told your whole life is looking for a feeling.

Dating really is this simple. It is knowing the characteristics of the person you want to be a partner to you. What do you want them to be like? Compassionate? Kind? Gentle? What are some things you want to avoid? Domineering? Anger issues? Stuck on themselves? And so, you want an idea of exactly what you're looking for so you know when you find it.

But assuming you have the maturity to be a good spouse, assuming you are what somebody else is looking for, you meet someone who meets those characteristics, you spend time with them (which is what we call dating) solely for the purpose confirming they meet the criteria.

You want to see them in different circumstances to make sure you're not getting duped. Make sure there's nothing crazy there that you're not unaware of. And then you commit to being a life partner to them. To ministering with them. The feelings are going to come and go, the attraction is going to come and go, the chemistry is going to change because people change throughout life. You want to make sure that faith is there, and once you confirm it's there, you shake hands and say let's do this thing for the rest of our lives.

And the added bonus, we get to be naked and make love. And that's the cherry on top. It just looks like that which is so very different than how the world does it.

Purity

Me: So, let's talk about purity. This has been one of the most common things I've talked about when it comes to singleness. Single people say, "Man, I can't wait until I'm married. I understand I won't have sex all the time, but I'm going to be able to have sex sometime. I'll be able to have at least some kind of sexual release. And right now, I'm not married, so when I have the urge, that's not something I can act on."

As single people, we know purity is always something we're going to struggle with, but won't it get easier once I'm married?

JP: Purity is a lot harder when there is a woman next to you who is unavailable to you. And that may be because she has the flu or COVID, it could be because she's uncomfortable because she's on her cycle, or she's nine months' pregnant. It could be for a variety of reasons.

I can't tell you how many people I've counseled who have gotten married and they weren't able to have sex for the first year of their marriage. There are some real challenges single people can be naive to.

Most people get married though, and they're able to have sex. And generally speaking, most people, if not everyone, will get married, and there will be times they want it, and it won't be available. And purity in those moments can be really, really challenging. Probably the time that it's the most challenging.

Me: I've talked to some married friends who have told me there will be aspects of purity that will be easier once you're married. But they encourage me to continue to fight like heck for purity now, because once you're married, there will be aspects of purity that won't just be harder but also new. There will be things you'll have to fight for in marriage that you never had to fight for as a single person.

I think we, as single people, don't know what we don't know about marriage. Have you seen marriage offer new challenges in purity that singleness never offered?

JP: Yes, of course. And I don't mean that in a belittling way, but as I listen to this question, I just kept thinking, "Of course!" Think about it. Let's say you're married, and you're having sex twice a week. You live with them, they're changing in front of you, you share a bathroom with them, you share a shower with them, and then you go on a business trip for a week.

All of a sudden that's not there anymore. The reason why it's important to keep sex in marriage and to keep marriage sacred is because marriage is the only place sex is safe. And anybody who will go outside of marriage for sex, including before they're married, is communicating, "Hey, I'm willing to go outside of marriage for sex." And that same person is on a business trip, sitting at the lobby bar, and the waitress walks up and starts talking. She says she gets off at nine and asks if you want to hang out afterward. That's super exciting. You're in a different city. Nobody is going to know.

Is that a greater temptation than waking up at 2:00 a.m. and wanting to look on my phone at Instagram or something? Absolutely it is. One hundred percent. It's a much bigger temptation.

And the only way I know I can pass that test is if I've passed the Instagram test or the pornography test or the sex before marriage test.

Older Singles Who Believe God Doesn't Have Anybody for Them

Me: There have been a wide variety of single people I've been able to meet in the process of writing this book. Some are older and have been on the receiving end of bad advice. "Just be patient, they're coming." "I went through a breakup a lot like yours right before I met my spouse. Don't worry."

And then some years pass. Still no one. And they now believe God doesn't have anyone for them. How would you counsel those people?

JP: That's hard because there's different people with different circumstances. But let's say it's you and you're feeling hopeless. Bro, I could find a girl you could be engaged to by Friday. I can't promise you that you'll be attracted to her or that you'll even like her. I don't know if she's going to meet your preferences. If you just desire marriage, I can find you a girl by Friday.

I think it's really an issue of preference and that's the challenge. Show me any girl, and there's guys out there who would love to marry that girl. She may not like them, and they may not meet her preferences. That's where it gets really complicated.

It's also not bad advice to tell someone not to worry because they went through a similar thing right before they met their spouse. It's just experience. It's true, which is why they're sharing it. And sometimes it happens, but the problem is sometimes it doesn't happen. When we start sharing our experience as if it's a certainty for somebody else, that's where it can set them up for discouragement.

I don't like the language, "What if God doesn't have somebody for me?" The truth is, for any given person, God has lots of people for them. They may not like them. But if they are a mature follower of Jesus, there are a lot of mature followers of Jesus they could marry.

Preferences rob us of paradise. Am I saying preferences don't have a place? No. They do have a place, but they shouldn't have first place. Things like attraction, chemistry, compatibility. Those things are most important to us, but they are *not* most important to God.

Single Women Wondering What They're Doing Wrong

Me: There have been some single people I've met who have told me they haven't been asked out in years. It's not that they're picky, but they haven't had the opportunity to be picky. And they ask me what they're doing wrong.

And since they ask me this question, I'll ask you the same question. What are they doing wrong, JP? Do they need to change anything? Do they need to get on some dating websites?

JP: I don't know that you're doing anything wrong. But if you're drawing a conclusion that you're doing something wrong because you're still single, that's what I would say you're doing wrong. So maybe the only thing you're doing wrong is drawing bad conclusions.

Should you be more bold? You can. You have the prerogative. Should you go on dating sites? You can. I don't know if you should. You can if you want to. If you're, like, I want to be married and I'm willing to do all things to get there, those are definitely things that will increase the potential of your getting married. Don't hope in those things.

But what was Jesus doing wrong? What was Paul doing wrong? They were single. We know in Jesus' case he didn't do anything wrong. And so maybe one of the things you're doing wrong is putting too much emphasis on marriage.

Matthew 19 says singleness is a high calling. First Corinthians 7 says singleness is a high calling. So maybe what you're doing wrong is not trusting God's Word. But there's also nothing wrong with desiring marriage. Just know that the world is fallen. Some people desire marriage, and they walk out their front door, get hit by a meteor, and they die. Or, worse, they trip and fall and break their neck and they're quadriplegic for the rest of their life. So, because the world is fallen, there are all kinds of outcomes. We don't need to draw conclusions from those outcomes, that it happened because of something. It may have just happened because of Genesis 3.

Can Single Guys and Single Girls Be Friends?

JP: It depends on what you mean by friends. I'm a huge fan of single followers of Jesus hanging out together in groups all the time. Experiencing community. That is right and true. Lots of single friends who love Jesus sitting in living rooms together and watching shows or movies together, playing games together, going on trips together, and being great friends.

Jesus hung out with Mary and Martha. They were great friends of his. So, if Jesus was friends with women, I can't be the one to say not to be. But you have to be wise. There are principles you need to apply to it. If it's a one-on-one best-friend situation, usually one of the hearts is drifting toward the other. And that's foolishness.

Loneliness

Me: There are people I have talked to who say that some of their most lonely days were in singleness. They found their spouse and loneliness went away. Then there are people I have talked to who say their most lonely nights have been lying in bed next to their spouse. What are your thoughts about loneliness in singleness and marriage? Does loneliness go away when you get married?

JP: I have felt loneliness in regard to wanting friendships and relationships. Monica is an introvert, and she never really feels lonely.

And just speaking to you, you have to initiate. So many people wait for others to call to invite them to come over.

Work through your contact list and say, "Do you guys want to come over?" "Hey, Susie, want to go bowling?" "Do you want to try this new coffee shop?" "Anybody want to play Go Fish?" That could be every Friday night for the rest of your life. So, I think a lot of times loneliness can be a lack of initiative.

But also, we talk about that 50 percent divorce rate. Man, that represents some deep sadness that has a lot of overlap with loneliness for sure.

So, I believe loneliness exists for single people and married people alike.

Me: You talk about the difference between you and Monica. She's an introvert and you're an extrovert. Is that hard for married people to navigate those differences?

JP: I would say it is one of the most challenging things in our marriage. I love to go and go and go, and she loves to stay at home. Staying at home is never fun for me. It's not my safe place. That is an area where we have to constantly compromise. It's been extremely challenging through the years for sure.

What About People Who Hate Their Singleness

Me: Is it okay to feel really bummed out about singleness? What about the people who have bought this book and just want to burn it instead of read it?

JP: Scripture says, "Godliness with contentment is great gain" (1 Tim. 6:6). So, I think to be discontent is a sin. God is gracious, though. *I think there's probably more discontented married people than discontented single people.*

In the same way that it is sinful to be discontent in marriage, it's sinful to be discontent in singleness. But I don't think longing for a spouse is sinful because the Bible says, "He who finds a wife finds a good thing and obtains favor from the Lord" (Prov. 18:22). And so, we can want things while we're being content, but when we see those things as ultimate and believe it's better than our current situation, then we're probably missing out on God's blessing.

Singleness is a gift. It's a sin to see it as anything but what the Scripture says. Children are a blessing from the Lord, so it's sinful to see children as anything but a blessing.

My hamartiology (study of sin) says that sin is less than God's best. It's missing the mark. I think there's a lot of things we do that are sinful and that's what makes me so thankful for grace through Jesus Christ.

What Would You Say to Single People?

JP: I have often heard the church handle Valentine's Day with everything from dismissive humor to great empathy. Admittedly, I've been a part of both.

If there is sadness for anyone who is single on Valentine's Day, I wonder what role the church has played in that. I think we have elevated marriage at the expense of devaluing singleness. As Christians, obviously the one we follow was single when he lived on Earth. For thirty-three years he never experienced sexual intimacy.

Marriage teaches us about submission and sacrifice. Those are the two primary lessons learned in marriage, and they are tools for our sanctification. I think we often think marriage will teach us about snuggling and sex. If you have a healthy sex life, you will do that 0.45 percent of the time. So, you will want to be really good at the submission and sacrifice that will happen the other 99.55 percent of the time.

While we learn some important lessons through marriage, singleness teaches us about the supremacy of

Jesus. Paul describes his singleness as a gift. It allowed him the freedom to pursue his first love of Jesus. Before we roll our eyes at Paul, we should know that he learned to value singleness from Jesus. In Matthew 19:12, Jesus says there are some who must be celibate for the sake of the kingdom, but then there are others who choose to. While not everyone can, those who can should. It seems to me that message is often not taught today.

Single friends, I'm sorry. The world has sold you on the idea that sex is the ultimate experience of life. The church has sold you that marriage is ideal. Some of you have a false view of marriage and need to hear that it is really hard. Most people fail at it. Others of you are afraid of marriage and you need to hear that marriage is really good. It, too, is a gift. I'm not sure if you need to hear that it is hard or it is good, but please listen accordingly. But my primary message to you is that singleness is good. Learn to appreciate the gift rather than resent it.

Chapter 11

Check, Please!

A few years ago, I decided to watch *The Office* all the way through for the first time. It took me awhile to get there because everyone kept telling I *needed* to watch it. So that meant I wasn't going to watch it. Don't tell me what to do, you know?

It took a few episodes, but eventually I was hooked. It seemed like everything I did revolved around getting to watch a few more episodes. I went home for lunch so I could watch a couple of episodes while I ate (my bank account also loved *The Office* as much as I did). I would wake up earlier some mornings to watch a couple of episodes. I would stay up late most nights because I told myself, "I can watch one more."

I loved it. I couldn't get enough of it. I felt like these were people I worked with. Jim was my best friend, Michael was my boss, and Karen would eventually be my girlfriend. Then the inevitable happened: the series finale. When the final episode ended, I just sat on the couch and stared at the end credits. Sadness overwhelmed me. Now what? What am I going to watch when I come home for lunch now? What do I do on my days off now? What do I do before I go to bed now? And the answer was, "That's it." These people weren't real. *The Office* wasn't an actual workplace. Jim wasn't my best friend, and Karen was too old for me even ten years ago when *The Office* was in production, so she's definitely too old for me now. It's done. Moving on to something else.

You've been on a journey over the last ten chapters. I pray you found some hope, purpose, meaning, and answers. I pray you fell more deeply in love with our Jesus. But whenever books like this one end, it always leads me to ask, "Now what?"

I felt that at the end of *The Office*. But can I tell you something? The answer to that question is very different for you at the end of reading this book than it was for me at the end of watching *The Office*. Singleness is very real. The answers aren't found in the pages of this book, but they are found in living them out after you close this book. Now what? Now the real journey begins.

Single people, let's go. Stop waiting and start acting. One of the things I struggle with the most is using my gift of singleness when I don't feel like it's a gift. It shows my immaturity, but my feelings often dictate my obedience. Singleness is a gift no matter what our feelings may be in that moment.

The only way God won't use our singleness is if we sit on the sideline and sulk. Honestly, our not using our gift of singleness doesn't just show our immaturity, it is incredibly revealing of our selfishness.

Yes, God has given us a gift to wreak havoc for the kingdom, but really what he has done is give us a gift to use to love the people he loves so much. He loved them so much he willed us to be single so we can reach out through grace to show them the scandalous love of God. He chose you and he chose me to be the person he uses to pursue other people, but most of the time we aren't faithful to that mission. Why? Because we don't like what it says after our relationship status? I know this won't be fun to hear, but how selfish is it for us not to be the vessel God uses to be his hands and feet to somebody who desperately needs it because we don't like the way we feel?

It's not immaturity that keeps us sidelined. It's selfishness.

And do you know how amazing God is? When we faithfully use our gift, we not only impact other people, but it's there that we find our purpose. It's there we find our meaning. It's when we start using our gift that we start seeing our gift as exactly that: a gift.

What a concept. Feeling like your singleness isn't a gift but a curse? Start using it. Stop waiting for your life to begin.

Life's too short. Yes, it is, but I think it's even shorter than we think it is. Our days are numbered (Job 14:5), and at any moment our number could be called. And when it's called, that's it. No do-overs. Not five more minutes. No opportunity to tie up loose ends. When our number is called, we will be face-to-face with our Creator and Savior. How have we lived? Will we be a war hero who wreaked havoc for the kingdom or someone who decided to play it safe on the sideline? I think single people a lot of times don't have a sense of purpose, not because singleness is purposeless, but because sideline (pew) sitting and passive waiting is purposeless and deeply lifeless.

We have been given a purpose that will always and forever be the same. The war we wage against the enemy and the kingdom he's trying to build is terrifyingly real. Souls are at stake.

Singleness isn't always easy. It can be lonely, frustrating, and often very confusing. But it has incredible purpose. No, let me rephrase it. *Single people have incredible purpose.* It's a powerful weapon God gives his single children to fight in the war. It's sharp and dangerous and it's designed to brutally harm Satan. It's time to stop viewing it as a weapon God is using to harm us.

Is it scary? You bet it is. But the gates of hell shake when it's used. The question shouldn't be *if* we're going to use it but *how* and *where* we're going to use it.

A few Sundays ago, we as a body were singing "O Praise the Name." The last verse in the song says, "He shall return in robes of white / The blazing sun shall pierce the night / And I will rise among the saints / My gaze transfixed on Jesus' face."

A thought came to my mind when we sang that verse. I have said multiple times in this book that the purpose of singleness isn't to prepare us for marriage. *Maybe I'm wrong. Maybe singleness does prepare us for marriage.*

"My gaze transfixed on Jesus' face." I thought about that for a moment. My life is in the rearview mirror. All the heartache. All the celebration. All the confusion. Everything on earth is but a memory, including death itself. It's all in the past. And there's Jesus, my future. The person I will be married to for eternity. The marriage that fully satisfies now and will never stop satisfying. A marriage that is a blood-bought promise. Now, that's a check that you can write, that God will always cash.

I fight the fight and run the race no matter my relationship status for that moment. For my Jesus. And no matter what happens, no matter the suffering, or if my relationship status ever changes, it would have all been worth it.

Single people, let's pick up our swords.

No more waiting.

No more searching for something in a marriage that is already in the palm of our hands right now.

It's time to fight. Our future spouse awaits us at the end of the battle. He is our reward. And he will always and forever be enough.

It's time to ask for the check at our table for one. The journey begins now.